The Spirits of '76

Books by HANS HOLZER

Ghost Hunter
Ghosts I've Met
Yankee Ghosts
Ghosts of the Golden West
Life After Death
The Prophets Speak
The Aquarian Age
The Phantoms of Dixie
The Power of Hypnosis
Haunted Hollywood
The Lively Ghosts of Ireland
The Great British Ghost Hunt
Gothic Ghosts

HANS HOLZER

The Spirits of '76

A Psychic Inquiry into the *American Revolution*

The Bobbs-Merrill Company, Inc.
Indianapolis / New York

COPYRIGHT © 1976 BY HANS HOLZER

All rights reserved, including the right to reproduce this book, or parts thereof, in any form, except for the inclusion of brief quotations in a review.

Published by the Bobbs-Merrill Company, Inc.
Indianapolis/New York

MANUFACTURED IN THE UNITED STATES OF AMERICA

Library of Congress Cataloging in Publication Data

Holzer, Hans W   1920–
   The spirits of '76.

   Includes index.
   1. Spiritualism—United States.   2. Ghosts—
United States.   3. United States—History—Revolution,
1775–1783—Miscellanea.   I. Title.
BF1311.U5H64   133.9   75-326901
ISBN 0-672-51884-8

Contents

Foreword [vii]

Chapter 1
The Peace Conference That Failed [1]

Chapter 2
Charlottesville and the Revolution [12]

Chapter 3
Michie Tavern, Jefferson, and the Boys [39]

Chapter 4
A Visit with the Spirited Jefferson [47]

Chapter 5
*A Revolutionary Corollary:
Patrick Henry, Nathan Hale, et al.* [59]

Chapter 6
The Philipsburg Manor Ghost [73]

Chapter 7
Major André and the Question of Loyalty [86]

Chapter 8
Benedict Arnold's Friend [118]

Chapter 9
The Haverstraw Ferry Case [136]

Chapter 10
A Visit to Oley Forge [152]

Chapter 11
The Lady from Long Island [170]

Foreword

Some years ago I opened exciting new vistas on historical research by developing a method known as historical psychometry. I would take psychic individuals, mediums, and sensitives to reputed historical "hot spots," to places where great events in history had transpired and where something from the past might presumably still cling to the environment. Of course I did this without telling my sensitive anything about the mission, or the circumstances, or, in fact, anything at all as to why we were visiting a certain place. The results were gratifying, to say the least. In a book titled *Window to the Past* I was able to pinpoint with great accuracy the actual Viking landing on Cape Cod and the real location of Camelot, and, in addition, to shed new light on the assassination of President Lincoln. I did this not on the say-so of my mediums, primarily Sybil Leek and Ethel Johnson Meyers, but as the result of follow-ups, traditional historical research emerging from the exciting new leads, and hints supplied by my psychic associates.

This method is based on the assumption that emotional events leave a fine imprint on their immediate surroundings in the nature of an electromagnetic field in which the principal events are recorded. In a way it is like an invisible motion picture, a two-dimensional record of happenings from the past. The imprint loses very little energy in the course of time, and though it may eventually fade, in terms of our lives the imprint may be considered indelible and permanent. Consequently, any talented psychic should be able to pick up all or part of such imprints and retell them, limited only by his or her own abilities to serve as a proper channel of communication.

In visiting historically active areas, be they buildings or monuments or simply outdoor sites where events have taken place in the past, the parapsychologist-historian comes face to face with two different phenomena. There is, first of all, the imprint from the past, a lifeless but nevertheless very accurate reproduction of something that has already taken place and is no longer taking place, is no longer of emotional impact to anyone. This two-dimensional imprint is, as already explained, sensed by the medium and retold to me, the investigator, with whatever degree of accuracy the sensitive is capable of. It is possible for such imprints to be visual as well as invisible. To a clairvoyant person, shades of past human beings become "visible" again simply because some part of the human personality remains behind in the atmosphere long after the physical body and even the etheric self have gone on. This should not be confused with earthbound spirits, commonly called ghosts, who remain behind in a place where some traumatic event, usually involving their demise, has taken place. This, then, is the second kind of phenomenon one may encounter in such emotionally impregnated areas. Whenever someone dies under tragic, traumatic, or somehow unacceptable conditions, or is unaware of his death and his passing into the next dimension, the phenomenon commonly called ghosts may occur. Only a small percentage of those who die violently, those who die under conditions that may be termed unexpected, become "hung up" entities, however. The majority, nevertheless, pass on to the next dimension without difficulty. The small number of individuals who cannot adjust to the afterlife and somehow remain behind in the physical atmosphere, although no longer part of it, can be observed at times by those with sufficient psychic abilities to sense them. If the emotional residue is strong enough to create three-dimensional projections, even those with minimal E.S.P. abilities may observe them. The degree of intensity of apparitions differs from case to case and from observer to observer.

In taking my psychic associates to places where tragic events in the past have occurred, I also opened the door to possible contact with such "hung up" personalities from the past—firstly, in the hope that my sensitives would see or hear them and describe them to me, and secondly, in the case of trance mediums, that the entities themselves might take advantage of the opportunity offered and speak to me directly through the intermediary of the entranced medium. In those cases I would be able to interrogate them directly, establish their identities, and perhaps learn more about their tragedies and problems than I could indirectly from the impressions gathered by mediums not capable of deep trance mediumship.

In the following pages I have employed all three methods,—clairvoyance, clairsentience and trance—when suitable. The subject is the Revolutionary War, the war which began in 1776 but which extended, at least in its implications, to the very end of the eighteenth century. I have visited locations intimately associated with the war itself and with the principals of that historical event.

In doing so I have kept in mind that battles and historical data are not the essence of man's progress in history. To the contrary, they are misleading at times because they need to be fleshed out by the human element, the motivations, the pros and cons, and the weaknesses and strengths of the leading characters, who alone emerge from the more intimate, personal investigation. Consequently, I have looked into the lives of both celebrated leaders of the Revolution and those who were merely onlookers, simple, private individuals without any claim to historical notoriety.

If anything, the results teach us that the people who suffered through the upheavals of that time were not so different from the people of today who must go through periods of violence and deprivation for one reason or another. Through it all there is an undertone of quiet pride in one's point of view, in one's cause, and a strong feeling that the world of tomorrow will be infinitely better than the present, with its trials and tribulations. Again, the parallels with today cannot be overlooked. The Revolution of 1776 pared the body politic of its excess fat of corruption, tyranny, and greed; two hundred years later, the evolution of 1976 should do likewise for the country.

Those who do not take the trouble to read these pages carefully, but skim through them, should not imagine that I have called on the spirits of George Washington, Benjamin Franklin, Benedict Arnold, et al., and conversed with them the way one does on the telephone. I have not deluded myself that I have listened to the voices of the dead without adequate proof that they are indeed authentic imprints from past events. *The Spirits of '76* is not a superficial fun book but the result of a prolonged and scientifically accurate investigation into psychic residues stemming from the American Revolution. As such, it may contribute additional and startling material to the historical perspective of that important event and, at the very least, bring today's reader in touch with the living past, not from musty history books, but from the faithful transcripts of recent investigations in places which saw history in the making.

HANS HOLZER

The Spirits of '76

1

The Peace Conference That Failed

In this age of peace conferences that go on for years and years without yielding tangible results—or, if any, only piecemeal ones, reached after long deliberation—it is a refreshing thought to remember that a peace conference held on Staten Island between Lord Howe, the British commander in America, and a congressional committee consisting of Benjamin Franklin, John Adams, and Edward Rutledge lasted but a single day—September 11, 1776, to be exact.

The position was this: the British were already in command of New York, Long Island and Staten Island, and the Yankees still held New Jersey and Pennsylvania, with Philadelphia as the seat of the Continental Congress. In view of his tremendous successes in the war against the colonists, Lord Howe felt that the suppression of the independence movement was only a matter of weeks. Wanting to avoid further bloodshed and, incidentally, to save himself some trouble, he suggested that a peace conference be held to determine whether an honorable peace could be concluded at that juncture of events.

Congress received his message with mixed emotions, having but lately worked out internal differences of opinion concerning the signing of the Declaration of Independence. A committee was appointed consisting of the aforementioned three men and empowered to investigate the offer. The three legislators went by horse to Perth Amboy, New Jersey, and were met at the New Jersey shore by a barge manned by British soldiers under a safe-conduct pass across the bay. They landed on the Staten Island shore and walked up to Bentley Manor, the residence of Lord Howe. There they were met with politeness and courtesies but also with a display of British might, for there were soldiers in full battle dress lined up along the road.

Later, the flamboyant John Adams told of soldiers "looking as fierce as ten furies, and making all the grimaces and gestures and motions of their muskets, with bayonets fixed, which, I suppose, military etiquette requires, but which we neither understood nor regarded."

Lord Howe outlined his plan for a settlement, explaining that it was futile for the Americans to carry on the war and that the British were willing to offer peace with honor. Of course, any settlement would involve the colonies' remaining under British rule. The three envoys listened in polite silence, after which Benjamin Franklin informed Lord Howe that the Declaration of Independence had already been signed on July 4, 1776, and that they would never go back under British rule.

The conference broke up, and Lord Howe, still very polite, had the trio conveyed to Amboy in his own barge, under the safe-conduct pass he had granted them. The following day,

The Peace Conference That Failed

September 12, 1776, the war of independence entered a new round: the Yankees knew what the British government was willing to offer them in order to obtain peace, and they realized that they might very well win the war with just a little more effort. Far from discouraging them, the failure of the peace conference on Staten Island helped reinforce the Continental Congress in its determination to pursue the war of independence to its very end.

This historical event took place in a manor house overlooking Raritan Bay, and at the time, and for many years afterward, it was considered the most outstanding building on Staten Island. The two-story white building goes back to before 1680 and is a colonial manor built along British lines. It was erected by a certain Christopher Billopp, a somewhat violent and hard-headed sea captain who had served in the British Navy for many years. Apparently, Captain Billopp had friends at court in London, and when the newly appointed Governor Andros came to America in 1674, he obtained a patent as lieutenant of a company of soldiers. In the process he acquired nearly one thousand acres of choice land on Staten Island. But Billopp got into difficulties with his governor and reentered navy service for a while, returning to Staten Island under Governor Thomas Dongan. In 1687 he received a land grant for Bentley Manor, sixteen hundred acres of very choice land, and on this tract he built the present manor house. The Billopp family were fierce Tories and stood with the crown to the last. The Captain's grandson, also named Christopher, who was already born in the manor, lived there till the end of the Revolution, when he moved to New Brunswick, Canada, along with many other Tories who could not stay on in the newly independent colonies.

From then on, the manor house had a mixed history of owners and gradually fell into disrepair. Had it not been built so solidly, with the keen eye of a navy man's perception of carpentry, perhaps none of it would stand today. As it was, an association was formed in 1920 to restore the historical landmark to its former glory. This has now been done, and the Conference House, as it is commonly called, is a museum open to the public. It is located in what was once Bentley Manor but today is called Tottenville, and it can easily be reached from New York City via the Staten Island Ferry. The ground floor contains two large rooms and a staircase leading to the upper story, which is also divided into two rooms. In the basement is a kitchen and a vaultlike enclosure. Both basement and attic are of immense proportions. The large room downstairs to the left of the entrance was originally used as a dining room and the room to the right as a parlor. Upstairs, the large room to the left is a bedroom while the one to the right is nowadays used as a Benjamin Franklin museum. In between the two large rooms is a small room, perhaps a child's room at one time. At one time there also was a tunnel from the vault in the basement to the water's edge, which was used as a means of escape during Indian attacks, a frequent occurrence in pre-colonial days. Also, this secret tunnel could be used to obtain supplies by the sea route without being seen by observers on land.

As early as 1962 I was aware of the Conference House and its reputation of being haunted. My initial investigation turned up a lot of hearsay evidence, hardly of a scientific nature, but nevertheless of some historical significance inasmuch as there is usually a grain of truth in all legendary stories. According to the local legends, Captain Billopp had jilted his fiancée, and she had died of a broken heart in the house. As a result, strange noises, including murmurs, sighs, moans, and pleas of an unseen voice, were reported to have been heard in the house as far back as the mid-nineteenth century. According to the old Staten Island newspaper *The Transcript*, the phenomena were heard by a

The Peace Conference That Failed

number of workmen during the restoration of the house after it had been taken over as a museum.

My first visit to the Conference House took place in 1962, in the company of Ethel Johnson Meyers and two of her friends, Rose de Simone and Pearl Winder, who had come along for the ride since they were interested in the work Mrs. Meyers and I were doing. Mrs. Meyers, of course, had no idea where we were going or why we were visiting Staten Island. Nevertheless, when we were still about a half hour's ride away from the house, she volunteered her impressions of the place we were going to. When I encouraged her to speak freely, she said that the house she had yet to see was white, that the ground floor was divided into two rooms, and that the east room contained a brown table and eight chairs. She also stated that the room to the west of the entrance was the larger room of the two, and that some silverware was on display in that room.

When we arrived at the house, I checked these statements at once; they were entirely correct, except that the number of chairs was seven, not eight as Mrs. Meyers had stated. I questioned the resident curator about this seeming discrepancy. One of the chairs and the silverware had indeed been on display for years but had been removed from the room eight years prior to our visit.

"Butler," Mrs. Meyers mumbled as we entered the house. It turned out that the estate next to Bentley belonged to the Butlers; undoubtedly, members of that family had been in the Conference House many times. As is my custom, I allowed my medium free rein of her intuition. Mrs. Meyers decided to settle on the second story room to the left of the staircase, where she sat down on the floor for want of a chair.

Gradually entering the vibrations of the place, she spoke of a woman named Jane whom she described as being stout, white haired, and dressed in a dark green dress and a fringed shawl. Then the medium looked up at me and, as if she intuitively knew the importance of her statement, simply said, "Howe." This shook me up, since Mrs. Meyers had no knowledge of Lord Howe's connection with the place she was in. I also found interesting Mrs. Meyers's description of a "presence," that is to say, a ghost, whom she described as a big man in a fur hat, being rather fat and wearing a skin coat and high boots, a brass-buckled belt, and black trousers. "I feel boats around him, nets, sailing boats, and I feel a broad foreign accent," Mrs. Meyers stated, adding that she saw him in a four-masted ship of a square-rigger type. At the same time she mentioned the initial T. What better description of the Tory, Captain Billopp, could she have given!

"I feel as if I am being dragged somewhere by Indians," Mrs. Meyers suddenly exclaimed, as I reported in my original account of this case in my first book, *Ghost Hunter*. "There is violence, and somebody dies on a pyre of wood. Two men, one white, one Indian; and on two sticks nearby are their scalps." It seemed to me that what Mrs. Meyers had tuned in on were remnants of emotional turmoil in the pre-colonial days; as I have noted, Indian attacks were quite frequent during the early and middle parts of the eighteenth century.

When we went down into the cellar, Mrs. Meyers assured us that six people had been buried near the front wall during the Revolutionary War and that they were all British soldiers. She also said that eight more were buried somewhere else on the grounds, and she had the impression that the basement had been used as a hospital during an engagement. Later investigation confirmed that members of the Billopp family had been buried on the grounds near the road and that British soldiers might very well have been buried there too, since there were frequent skirmishes around the house from July 1776 to the end of the year. Captain Billopp was twice kidnapped from his own house by armed bands operating from the New Jersey shore.

It was clear to me that Mrs. Meyers was entering various layers of history and giving us bits and pieces of her impressions, not necessarily in the right order but as she received them. The difficulty with trance mediumship is that you cannot direct it the way you want to, that is to say, ferret out just those entities or layers from the past you are interested in. You have to take "pot luck," as it were, hoping that sufficient material of interest will come through the medium.

Once more we returned to the upper part of the house. Suddenly Mrs. Meyers turned white in the face and held on for dear life to the winding staircase. For a moment she seemed immobilized. Then, coming to life again, she slowly descended the stairs and pointed to a spot near the landing of the second story. "A woman was killed here with a crooked knife!" she said.

Aha, I thought, there is our legend about Captain Billopp and his jilted fiancée. But he didn't kill her; she had died of a broken heart. Mrs. Earley, the custodian, was trying to be helpful, so I questioned her about any murder that might have occurred in the house. "Why, yes," she obliged. "Captain Billopp once flew into a rage and killed a female slave on that very spot on the stairs." As she spoke, I had the impression that the custodian was shuddering just a little herself.

From time to time people had told me of their visits to the Conference House and wondered whether the "ghost in residence" was still active. Finally I asked a young lady I had been working with for some time to try her hand at picking up whatever might be left in the atmosphere of the Conference House. Ingrid Beckman, an artist by profession, knew very little about the house but had access to the short account of my investigation given in *Ghost Hunter*.

I asked Ingrid to go to the house by herself, and on the afternoon of November 25, 1972, she paid it a visit.

In order to avoid tourists, she had arrived at the house about one o'clock. The house was still closed to visitors so she sat down on a bench outside. "I walked around, and even on the outside I felt a presence," Ingrid began her report to me. "I felt as if the place were really alive. Then I went up to the front porch and peeked into the main hallway, and when I looked up the stairs I had a feeling of gloom and foreboding. I had the distinct sensation of a dangerous situation there."

Strangely enough, Ingrid seemed to have been led to that house. Two weeks prior to her visit, she had happened to find herself in Nyack, browsing through some antique shops. There she met a woman who started to talk to her. The woman explained that she was from Staten Island, and when she discovered that Ingrid lived there also, she suggested that Ingrid visit a certain house, once the property of an old sea captain. The house, the lady said, had an interesting tunnel which began behind a fireplace and ran down to the water's edge. Ingrid, always interested in visiting old houses, had promised to look into the matter. This was two weeks before I mentioned a visit to the Conference House to her.

The following weekend, Ingrid was with some friends at her apartment on Staten Island. She took the opportunity of asking whether any of them had ever heard of the house as described by her acquaintance. One of the young men present affirmed that there was such a house, called the Conference House, and that it was haunted by the spirit of a slave who had been killed there. That was on Sunday. The following Monday I telephoned Ingrid with the request to go to the Conference House.

As Ingrid was sitting on the front porch of the house, waiting for the door to be opened, she had the distinct feeling that someone was watching her. "I felt as if someone knew I was there," she explained, "and I especially felt this coming from the window above the hallway. It is a crooked window, and I felt that it had some sort of significance. If anyone were looking at me or wanted to get my attention, it would be through that window. But when I went in, as soon as the door had been opened to visitors, the first place I went to was the basement. As I was looking around the basement, I came upon a little archway, as if I had been *directed* to go there."

The spot made her literally jump; she felt that something terrible had occurred near the fireplace, and she experienced heavy chills at the same time; someone had been brutalized at the entrance to the tunnel. Fortunately, she had managed to go there by herself, having discouraged the tourist guide from taking her around. "The tunnel entrance is particularly terrorizing," Ingrid said. "This tunnel caused me chills all the way up to my neck."

Finally tearing herself away from the basement, she went up the stairs, again by herself. Immediately she arrived at the upper landing and went to the bedroom to the left; as she stood in the entranceway, she heard a noise like a knock.

"The hallway upstairs felt terrible," Ingrid explained. "I turned around and looked down the stairs. As I looked, I almost became dizzy. It felt as if someone had been pushed down them or hurt on them." To be sure that she wasn't imagining things or being influenced by what she had read, Ingrid decided to go up and down those stairs several times. Each time, the sensation was the same. On one of her trips up the stairs, she ascertained that the window, which had so attracted her while she was still waiting outside, was indeed just outside the haunted stairwell.

"I got the impression of a slave woman, especially in the upstairs bedroom; I also felt there was a disturbance around the table downstairs, but I don't think the two are connected. I felt the woman was associated with the upstairs bedroom and the stairway and possibly the tunnel entrance; but the feeling in the basement is another episode, I think."

"What period do you think the disturbances go back to?" I asked.

"I'd say the 1700s, going back before the Revolution."

"Do you have the feeling that there is still something there that hasn't been fully resolved?"

"Yes, definitely. I think that is why I had such strong vibrations about it, and I think that is also why I got the information two weeks beforehand."

"Do you think that it is a man or a woman who is 'hung up' in there?"

"I think it is a woman, but there may also be a man because the scene at the table had something to do with a man. He may have been shot, or he may have been abducted from that room—you know, taken through the tunnel."

I suddenly recalled that Captain Billopp was twice abducted by Yankee irregulars from the Jersey shore. Gabriel Disosway, in his 1846 account of the Manor of Bentley, reported that "Colonel Billopp, at the time a warm party man and military leader, was closely watched, and, it is said, was twice taken from his own house by armed bands from 'the Jerseys,' and thus made a prisoner. Amboy is in sight, and upon one of these occasions, he was observed by some Americans, who had stationed themselves with a spy glass in the church steeple of that town. As soon as they saw him enter his abode, they ran to their boats, rapidly crossed the river, and he was soon their captive."

On January 28, 1973, Ingrid made another, spontaneous visit to the Conference House. She had much the same impressions as before, but this time she managed to speak to the caretaker. The lady admitted hearing heavy footsteps upstairs at times, which sounded to her like those of a man wearing heavy boots with spurs attached. Also, on the anniversary of "the murder," the caretaker claims to have seen a man run up the stairs toward a girl waiting on the first landing. "Her story is that the girl was beheaded," Ingrid reported further. "She says that one afternoon last summer, as she was dusting the room on the left of the ground floor, she could put her hand 'right through' a British soldier! This past summer her daughter from South Carolina came to visit and insisted on staying upstairs in the haunted rooms. That night the daughter allegedly heard a man's laughter, followed by a woman's laughter, and then a shriek. According to the caretaker, this happens at regular intervals."

The caretaker's account fascinated me and would have been even more impressive had Ingrid not also overheard her telling some visiting tourists that I had visited the Conference House in the company of Orson Welles, Ethel Meyers, and Sybil Leek. Quite obviously, the good lady was confusing my mention of these three people in the same book, *Ghost Hunter*, with my relatively simple and short account of my visit to the Conference House. Under the circumstances, we can't be too sure about the footsteps and the woman's shriek in the night. What we can be sure of, however, is the very real, very tangible imprint of Lord Howe's fruitless discussion with Benjamin Franklin, John Adams, and Edward Rutledge. It is a good thing that these three signers of the Declaration of Independence did not stay the night as guests of Lord Howe. Imagine what would have happened if they had met up with the murdered slave girl on the stairs!

2

Charlottesville and the Revolution

When people think of the American Revolution, they think primarily of Boston and the Tea Party, Paul Revere and his ride, and Philadelphia and its Liberty Bell. Very few people realize that Charlottesville, Virginia, was the focal point of the emerging United States for a while—that it was at the little, conveniently situated town in northern Virginia that much of the early planning of the Revolution took place. That was so because some of the leaders of American independence, such as Thomas Jefferson and James Monroe, made their homes in and around Charlottesville. Foreign tourists who are eager to see Washington, D.C., and cannot get enough of its majestic government buildings should take an extra hour to fly down to Charlottesville to see where it all began.

I hadn't been to Charlottesville since 1964, when Horace Burr, professor of speech and director of drama at Madison College in Harrisonburg, Virginia, and Virginia Cloud, the noted librarian and historian, had invited me. At that time, however, my main interest was in ferreting out some of the local ghosts and discussing them in a book I was then writing. Professor Burr was instrumental in prearranging my visit in early February 1973, knowing what I was hoping for, and clearing permission for me and a mediumistic friend to visit some private homes of the area. Virginia Cloud was on hand too, and it felt like old times revisited when my friend Ingrid Beckman and I emerged from the jet plane at the little Charlottesville airport. We were going to stay for two days, which had been tightly planned by Professor Burr and Miss Cloud. Even a television interview with a crew from nearby Richmond, Virginia, had been penciled into the schedule, and I gave it while standing on the historical staircase of the Burr house, Carrsgrove.

Immediately upon arriving, we checked in at the Monticello Hotel in downtown Charlottesville. In retrospect, it seems odd that such a patently third-rate provincial hotel should bear the illustrious name of Monticello. The rooms weren't at all what we had ordered, the service and food were below standard, and it occurred to me how Jefferson would have felt had he been forced to put up some of his friends at this hostelry. Fortunately, it didn't exist during Jefferson's lifetime.

It turned out that February 9 was also Professor Burr's birthday, and he had accepted an invitation for the evening from the president of the University. Nevertheless, he spent the afternoon with us. Promptly at two o'clock, he picked us up at the hotel and, together with Miss Cloud, who had arranged our visit, drove us to Foxhill Farm, now the home of Mrs. Isabelle Palmer, a prominent society leader in Charlottesville. The house is somewhat on the outskirts of the town itself, on a knoll set back from the street. Although of pre-Revolutionary origin, it has been nicely fixed up and contains the latest comforts. Its dozen or so rooms are distributed on two floors, with a large kitchen downstairs and an imposing dining room to the right of the entrance. Upstairs, there are mainly bedrooms. Behind the house is the loveliest of gardens, enclosed by a brick wall behind which extend the rolling hills of Virginia's horse country, as far as the eye can reach.

Mrs. Palmer received us with much cordiality, and, as she had been briefed beforehand not to divulge anything about the house while Ingrid and I were inspecting it, only formalities and generalities were exchanged between us at first. As is my custom, I let my mediumistic associate go about the house as her intuition commanded her. Immediately on entering the large room to the right of the entrance, Ingrid stopped. She found herself now in the left-hand corner of what was obviously a dining room.

"What's the matter?" I asked, realizing that she was picking up some imprint from the past.

"I have a generally heavy feeling here. I can't describe it as yet, but the area is loaded with impressions," Ingrid replied, still trying to get her psychic bearings.

Ever since I had started to work with Ingrid, my own E.S.P. ability had also sharpened, and on occasion I was able to sense things along with her. Thus I heard myself say, "Walk around and see whether you feel anything. I get the feeling of a meeting of some importance having taken place here." I had no idea why I said it, but both Ingrid and I agreed that a meeting of some importance had taken place in that very room, that someone had been arguing and had gotten up to leave in order to warn someone about a matter of importance.

"I feel there is a series of meetings here, not just one," Ingrid added, and then we walked over to the kitchen area. Since Ingrid felt nothing particularly strong in that area, we proceeded upstairs.

As soon as Ingrid walked into the bedroom to the left of the stairs, she stopped. "Guests on government business stayed here," she said, touching the bed to receive stronger psychometric impressions. "I 'get' a woman here; she is the wife of someone who has gone away, and I think she is very anxious for him. I get the feeling that she is worried for the man to get through the lines, and she is sitting up in an all-night vigil."

While Ingrid was speaking, I received the impression of the name Margaret, followed by the initial L. I have no idea why, but the imprint was quite strong.

"I have the feeling a lot of people went up and down the front stairway in the middle of the night," Ingrid said, "and that this is in a sense like a refuge."

I turned to Mrs. Palmer and Horace Burr, asking them to comment on the psychic impressions received by Ingrid and myself.

"Well," Professor Burr began, "this house, Foxhill Farm, stood halfway between Brown's Cove and the new village of Charlottesville at the time of the Revolutionary War. Our civilization came in through this part, through the valley, along the river. So this was actually a very important location; people who lived here were well-to-do, and it was a huge plantation. The owner was a certain John Rodes, and his son David was made sheriff of the county in 1775. During colonial days, the post of sheriff was a very important government position, and Rodes had his own son filling that office.

"Since this house was a place halfway between the Revolutionary lines and the British, I felt it would be interesting to see what your psychic friend would get from the vibrations in the house," Burr added.

"What about the important meetings both Ingrid and I felt in the dining room downstairs?" I asked.

Professor Burr nodded emphatically. "Yes, if there were meetings they would undoubtedly have been held here."

At this point, Mrs. Palmer explained that the corner of the dining room where Ingrid had felt such strong vibrations had always puzzled her. It was on that spot that she had felt chills and had a sense of presence. Not being a medium, however, she could do very little with it. Nevertheless, she felt that whatever psychic activities might be present in her house would center around that corner of the dining room. I then questioned her about the room upstairs where Ingrid had had such a vivid impression. It turned out that the room was exactly above the library and not far from the area where the meetings had been held in the dining room. The house itself consisted originally of two separate houses that were joined together in the middle. The area where Ingrid had felt the strongest impressions had been built in 1765; the other, where she had felt nothing special, had been built in 1807.

I then directed a question to Burr. "Was there any particular meeting where people were sitting down at a long table, wearing a kind of severe dark brown coat, with lots of buttons running down the middle? Somebody at the end of the meeting would be getting up with a rather serious face, saying, 'I'll let him know,' and then take some papers and leave the assembly. This would have been very late at night or early in the morning, and someone would have to ride quite a distance to notify someone of a decision taken here for some area to join up with some other forces." As I finished speaking, I wondered where I had gotten all that information; it seemed to me that it was simply coming out of me, as if I had been *impressed* with it by some external source. I could tell by the look on Ingrid's face that she felt pretty much the same but that I had somehow expressed it first.

Burr thought this over for a moment. "It sounds very reasonable, since it was the time when they were recruiting and the sheriff would have had his hand in it, of course."

Again I followed a hunch. "Has anyone ever left here who was connected with this house and whose life was in jeopardy if he were caught?"

"Well, okay," Burr replied, "then let us go into the bloodstain on the floor, which you can see plainly even now." Sure enough, in the door jamb between the library and the next room there was a bloodstain deeply soaked into the wood.

Isabelle Palmer took up the explanation from this point on. "This has some connection with a Revolutionary person," she explained. "That is why when you mentioned refuge it hit home with me. Tradition has it that a wounded man came here during the Revolution and sought refuge. But we don't know who he was or whether he died here."

We walked back into the sumptuous library and sat down, surrounded by eighteenth-century oil paintings of great historical value. I asked about the men dressed in the reddish brown long coats which I had been impressed with a little while earlier. Could it have any meaning in terms of historical fact?

"Well," Burr replied, "that was the most typical homespun yarn that you could have in the 1770s in Piedmont, which is where we are. The material was produced on a loom and dyed with tobacco dyes, so the colors were dark brown."

Since the old pre-Revolutionary houses were once the centers of large plantations, they are not clustered in or around the town of Charlottesville but stand in lonely majesty in the countryside, even though much of the land has long since been sold off. Such was the case with Castalia, an imposing three-story manor house with red brick at the bottom, a veranda going around most of the house, and a portico dressing up the rest. The tall red brick chimneys, which supplied the fireplaces with outlets in the days before central heating, look like imposing flagpoles peering out into the Virginia hills. Castalia is surrounded by tall, old trees and is reached by a driveway from a dirt road which in turn branches off the main highway. Even in its reduced size, Castalia is the center of an estate which takes a full fifteen minutes to drive through.

As we were halfway between the town of Charlottesville and the estate, Virginia Cloud, who had been chatting incessantly, as is her custom, happened to say something about a ghost. Now, don't get me wrong. Virginia Cloud has a lot to say, and nothing she ever tells you is without interest. She probably knows more about motion pictures and stars than any living soul, and nearly everything there is to know about Charlottesville and the American Revolution.

"About that ghost," I said, and turned around. I was seated next to Horace Burr, and Ingrid and Virginia were in the rear seats.

"Well," Virginia said, "this very road we are riding on is the road where my friend Mrs. Emily Money Kelly had a remarkable experience with a ghost."

"Tell me more," I coaxed her, as if that were necessary.

"Emily lived nearby because her father was Colonel Money, an Englishman who worked for John Armstrong Chandler, a very famous gentleman of the area. One night Emily and her sister were on this long road which, as you know, connects Castle Hill with Castalia."

I knew that fact very well. In 1964 I had visited Castle Hill, where there is a haunted bedroom, allegedly visited at times by a lady ghost who appears only to people she doesn't like so she can tell them to leave "her" bedroom. At the time of my visit to Castle Hill, I had questioned the owner, Colonel Clark Lawrence, about any psychic occurrences. Politely, he informed me that he had none to report.

"Emily and her sister were turning into the driveway of their house, when they saw a rider very clearly—so clearly, in fact, that upon arriving at the door they asked one of their servants, 'Who was right in front of us when we came here?' The man seemed surprised. 'Why, Miss Emily, I've been out here all evening and I didn't see anybody.' Other people living in the area have also reported seeing a lonely rider ahead of them, heading up the road from Castle Hill to Castalia. Nobody knows who he is, or where he goes."

I thanked Virginia for her contribution to the local ghost lore, and just then the sleek blue car turned into the driveway leading up to Castalia. There we were welcomed by the owners, the Boocock family. We were exactly eighteen miles from Charlottesville and in the very heart of the Virginia horse country. The several ladies and gentlemen assembled to greet us in the large parlor downstairs were all members of the family, eager to contribute their experiences to the investigation. As I had requested that nothing be said about the house or the occurrences therein, only polite chitchat was exchanged at first. Ingrid took a look at the downstairs part of the house, and explained how pleasing it was to her artistic taste. But within a matter of minutes, she was on her way upstairs and I followed her, tape recorder and camera in hand. Behind me came Horace Burr and Virginia Cloud, followed at a respectful distance by the lady of the house.

The house was living proof that the Southern gentry still knows how to furnish homes. Elegantly decorated in the proper style, without so much as a single intrusion of modernism or so-called improvements, the interior of Castalia was a joy to the eye. Four-posters, heavy drapes, thick carpets, early nineteenth-century furniture, beautifully carved staircases and, above all, rooms upon rooms, space upon space, and all of it deep in the country, far away from pressures and the onrushing traffic.

As soon as we reached the second-floor landing, Ingrid made an immediate dash for a corner room, later identified as the chintz room. It had windows on both outside walls, giving a person an excellent view of the drive and thus of anyone coming up to the house. There was a period bed, or rather a double bed, in the center, and heavy drapes at the tall windows, reaching almost to the floor in the French manner. Opposite the bed stood a dresser with a large mirror. Horace and I kept back, close to the entrance door, while Ingrid walked slowly around the room.

"There is an impression here of an older woman; I get the feeling of an all-night vigil," she said finally. "I think she is worried about someone at a distance." I queried her about the person this woman worried over. "It is a man," Ingrid replied. "He's away on a war campaign. I think he is either a general or some other high-ranking officer; a leader and a patriot."

"Try to see what he looks like," I instructed her, "what his name is, what his connection is with this house, anything you can get on him."

Ingrid closed her eyes, breathed deeply for a moment, then reopened them again and said, "He is at a great distance right now, a hundred miles or more. She is worried that he may never return."

"Is he in any kind of action at the moment?"

"Yes. There is a decision, a turning point in the war, and she is worried that he may not come back from it. I get 1760 or '70. Her name is Margaret."

"What happened to this man? Does he come back?"

Ingrid's face took on a sad expression, almost as if she were feeling what "Margaret must have felt at the time. "I don't think he comes back."

"What happens to her?"

"She stays here in great sadness."

"Is she still attached to this house, or do you merely feel her imprint?"

"Oh, I think she comes here. I think this is the room where she did most of her worrying. She comes back in the hopes that *he* will return."

"Did he die in battle?"

"Yes."

"How did she hear of it?"

"A carrier came with the news."

"How is it connected with this house?"

"He owned it; he was in the family."

"When the news came to her, was she in this room?"

"Yes, she was ill."

"As you speak, do you sense her close to you? Is she in some way telling you this? What was she dressed like?"

"I think she wore a nightgown," Ingrid replied, closing her eyes again to better describe what her psychic senses told her. "She wears perfume, her hair is pulled back, it is of dark brown color. She's a woman of perhaps forty-five. She likes to wear flowered clothes, gauzy material, and beads around her neck."

"What keeps her in this house?"

"He never returned and she is *still waiting*."

"Is she aware of his death?"

"She's confused."

"Does she realize that her own death has occurred?"

"I don't think so."

Next, we entered the so-called lavender room, also on the second floor of the house. It was situated opposite the chintz room, on the right side of the stairwell, but also facing toward the road so that one could observe it from the window. The lavender room was considerably smaller than the chintz room we had just left. I decided to leave Ingrid and Virginia alone in it for a few moments, to see whether they could gather up some impressions from the past. Meanwhile, I went outside to change film and tape.

When I returned, both ladies seemed agitated and said they had news for me. "I think a woman was brought in here. She was very ill and stayed here until her death," Ingrid said firmly. "I think it is the same woman I felt in the chintz room except that she actually stayed in this one. I think she received the shock when she was in the other room, and then her condition became hopeless and she was moved in here. I don't know whether it was because of drink, but she never recovered emotionally. She was in here for several years, and eventually she died here. In this room I feel only sadness and the long-drawn-out period of her suffering. I think she wants to tell her story, she is so lonely and sad."

I instructed Ingrid to try and contact the entity, in trance if possible. Obediently, Ingrid sat back in a deep, comfortable chair in the corner, closed her eyes and waited. Although full trance did not occur, she seemed very much under the influence of an outside entity. "David," Ingrid said, her voice barely audible. "David or Davis," she added, "I think that is the man. She is very confused and still waiting for him." I instructed Ingrid to inform the lady that the man had passed on and that she herself was no longer in the flesh. Did the spirit understand her condition? "She understands what I am saying," Ingrid replied, "but I don't think she pays attention."

I decided to follow a different route of questioning. "Ask her to reveal more about herself."

"I think she was a very delicate lady, with lots of perfumes and fineries and beads; she catered to herself. She was a socially prominent woman."

"Was there anything among her habits that was particularly outstanding, such as a hobby or interest of some sort?"

"I think she liked to read a lot. Poetry. Especially Emerson, I think. But she didn't do any more reading after her loss; she was too confused. She thinks she is still here. *She is afraid to leave.*"

As is my custom under such circumstances, I explained to the entity that she could join her loved one merely by calling out to him and displaying a sincere desire to join him. Did the spirit lady understand what I was saying to her? "She listens," Ingrid explained. "She is showing herself to me with a shawl now, a white shawl bordered with fringes. Maybe she does needlework. She is always watching out the windows. *But the news does not come.* She grows old in this room."

"Does she understand why the man she is waiting for is not returning?"

"No. She is very stubborn."

But eventually, Ingrid and I persuaded her that there was no point in waiting any longer, and with our blessings we sent her away to the man who had also been waiting for her on *his* side of the road.

We continued our inspection of the large house, walking down half a flight of stairs and up another half on the other side of the house, which apparently had been built at a different time. The house presented a fascinating pattern of staircases and corridors, not laid out in a perfectly straight pattern but allowing for unexpected corners, turns, and hidden nooks. The master bedroom was located at the other end of the house, its windows looking down onto the land and toward the main road in the distance. It was a bright, large, and well-appointed room, beautifully decorated and well kept. Again, I let Ingrid step into it first by herself to pick up whatever she could in the way of psychic impressions.

"I don't feel anything here," Ingrid announced with a determined tone of voice. I had learned to respect her judgment, for whenever she felt nothing in the atmosphere of a room, there usually was nothing to be felt. On the other hand, whenever I had taken her to allegedly haunted rooms, she had picked up the scent without fail. I thanked her, and we descended to the ground floor, where the members of the family awaited us with great curiosity. Briefly, I filled them in on what Ingrid had discovered and in turn asked them to brief us on the house and make comments about Ingrid's discoveries.

Horace Burr was the first to speak. "The grandson of the famous Dr. Thomas Walker of Castle Hill, about whom you have written in *Ghosts I've Met*," he said, "had a grandson named Lewis. The house, as it stands now, was built around 1850, but there was an older house here before that time." Burr got up and showed me the dividing line where the old part ended and the newer portion began. About two-thirds of the living room was in the older section, while the frontal third actually occupied the newer part of the house. "So the first part, that is, the first room we were in, wasn't standing when the phenomena occurred," Burr explained. "Yet the apparition of a woman which has been observed by many of the people around here always occurred in the chintz room, the room where Ingrid correctly identified her. This was Mrs. Sally Lewis, the wife of Robert Lewis."

"Who saw her?" I asked.

"Mrs. Lila Boocock, the present Mrs. Boocock's sister-in-law. It happened prior to her marriage when she, her mother, and her intended were visiting here from New York. In the middle of the night, she was awakened by a little woman with dark brown hair, pulled back, wearing a *shawl* and a striped taffeta dress. The woman was in her bedroom busying herself with a briefcase which Lila had brought with her and which contained some real estate papers. *The ghostly lady tried to go through it as if she were checking things out.* As Lila sat in bed, amazed at what she saw, she heard a sound reminding her of crisp onions being cut while the woman was going through her papers. Finally the woman walked straight over to the bed, with a faint smile on her face, and leaned over as if she wanted to say something. *The next moment she was gone.*"

Mrs. Lila Boocock lives in Florida now. The experience occurred in 1926.

I turned to my hostess, Mrs. Elizabeth Boocock. "Have you yourself had an experience along these lines?"

"Yes," she replied. "Before we actually lived here, we used to come down to visit, and we would take the bedroom in the left part. That was in 1929. One morning I woke up around five o'clock because I heard footsteps with a regular rhythm to them. It sounded like, one-two-three-stop. At first I thought that my husband was ill. He hadn't been very well and was in the bed next to me, so I turned on the lights. But he was sound asleep. After that, I heard the same footsteps again and again, always at five o'clock in the morning. Finally I asked my mother-in-law what it all meant, and she replied, 'Oh, that's Mrs. Lewis.' But I never heard it again after we moved into the house."

I turned to the attractive lady to her right, Gwendolyn Goss, Mrs. Boocock's daughter, asking for any first-hand experiences.

"When I was at school in 1943, I brought a roommate home for Thanksgiving weekend," she began. "My friend, Marie de France, and I stayed in the chintz room, and it was a very cold, windy night, so we had a fire going in the fireplace. We put our clothes over a chair near the fireplace and went to bed. Sometime after midnight I heard some noise, as if someone were moving around the room, and I assumed Marie had gotten up. At the same time, Marie thought I had gotten up, so we both got out of bed and turned on the lights. Imagine our surprise when we found all our clothes on the floor *and the chair turned toward the fireplace with an open book on it!* Neither of us had put the book there. All that time the wind was blowing hard and the room was icy cold."

"Someone must have sat in that chair, reading a favorite book by the fireplace," I interjected. Horace Burr gave me a significant look.

"When we first moved down here, we lived in this house for a while before we moved out to the cottage, which you can see out the window," Gwendolyn continued. "When mother mentioned again and again to me that she had heard footsteps of an unseen person overhead, I finally said, 'Why, that's ridiculous.' But one night I heard the footsteps myself and immediately went upstairs to look. They sounded like four very definite footsteps going in one direction, then turning around and coming back. Immediately I went upstairs to look above the room I was in, and there was nothing."

"What sort of footsteps were they?" I asked.

"It sounded almost as if someone were pacing up and down," Gwendolyn replied.

"But that wasn't all," she continued. "During the 1930s my grandparents had gone to Europe for a while, and the house was locked up. Not only was it closed from the outside but each individual room in the house itself was also locked. When they sent word by cablegram that they were coming home and asked the maid and the farm manager to open the house for them, these people came in. When they got to the lavender room and unlocked the door, they found the bedspread off the bed and on the floor, the bureau scarf off it, and all the silver in a mess. It looked as if someone had gone through it in a fit of temper, yet there had been no one in the house. No one could have gotten in. A mouse couldn't have gotten in.

"On one occasion, Mrs. Boocock and her mother were sleeping

in the room next to the chintz room, when she heard a crash in the middle of the night which sounded to her as if someone had jerked off the dresser scarf and everything had gone to the floor. When the two women checked, they found everything in order. This happened two or three times in a row, both in the chintz room and in the lavender room."

"It would seem that somebody was looking for something, wouldn't it?" I said. "But I wonder who the ghost was waiting for?"

"I think I can answer that," Horace Burr said. "Mrs. Lewis's son had been hunting nearby when he shot himself accidentally, or so they say. That was in 1855. Naturally she was upset, pacing up and down, waiting for someone who never came. Ingrid mentioned someone who was part of the family, and she mentioned her reading Emerson. That would fit. George Lewis is buried here in the grounds."

A tall, heavy-set man who had been listening to the conversations in patience and silence spoke up now. He turned out to be Gwendolyn's husband, Edward Goss. Since he was an expert in engineering matters, he wanted us to know that important structural changes had taken place in the house. Both the lavender room and the chintz room had been changed, in 1904 and then again in 1909. He understood that the late Mrs. Sally Lewis was "unhappy" about the changes in her house. He explained that during the Revolutionary period there was a double cabin about two minutes away from the main house, and that this cabin was built in 1747 by a man named Jack, not far from the Castalia spring, which had been named after the legendary spring on Mount Parnassus.

"About two years after Lila Boocock had seen the apparition of Mrs. Lewis in her bedroom," Goss said, "she happened to be introduced to a granddaughter of the late Mrs. Lewis. After describing the apparition in detail, she asked the granddaughter whether she recognized it. 'That is my grandmother,' the granddaughter said firmly. 'She was little and had straight, pulled-back hair. She wore a shawl and a striped taffeta dress.' "

"Did you yourself ever have an experience in the house?"

"Yes, I did. In 1947 the then owner of the house, Mrs. Marmie Boocock, was away in Florida, and the house was quite empty except for myself. One night I noticed a light shining from a distance, and when I went up to investigate, I realized the light was coming from the chintz room. Sure enough, the lights had been turned on in that room. Since I had been the only one in the house and hadn't turned them on, there was no natural explanation for it."

I suddenly recalled that Ingrid had "gotten" the name Margaret when we had first entered the chintz room. Certainly Marmie and Margaret are close enough.

When we had first entered the house, I had asked Virginia Cloud to observe what she could, psychically speaking, and to make notes of her impressions. She too had a very strong impression in the chintz room of a woman named Louise, which of course, could have been Lewis. She "saw" her as a woman with white hair and blue eyes, wearing a kind of filmy nightgown, possibly with a cap on her head, and felt that she had lived quite a long time ago. Virginia sensed that the woman had some anxiety about another person *whom she also felt present in the room.* The other person Virginia thought was a very vital individual, and she "got" the name Henry or Alexander. Local tradition has had it that a restless spirit from another century lived on in the patrician rooms of Castalia. Is it a Revolutionary wraith, or indeed Mrs. Lewis, waiting for her beloved son to return from the hunt?

As we were about to leave, I noticed a book on the table in the library downstairs. It was *A Pride of Lions*, by Lately Thomas.

The book deals with the life of a local celebrity, John Armstrong Chandler. When Ingrid saw it, she let out a little cry. The book seemed to have been placed there, as if to greet her. You see, it was Ingrid who had designed the jacket for it.

The Farm is a most unlikely name for one of Charlottesville's oldest buildings. Actually, it is a handsome two-story brick house, with a prominent fireplace on one end. The downstairs is now divided into two rooms—a front room very much the way it was in colonial days, and a back room now used by the owner, the postmaster of Charlottesville, as a kind of storage room. Upstairs are two bedrooms. The house stands in a tree-studded lot right in the very center of Charlottesville. A little to the left of the house, the postmaster pointed out the spot where the old Kings Highway used to go through. It was here also that Ingrid felt the vibration of many men passing by.

On the outside of The Farm, a simple plaque reminds visitors that this is one of the most historical spots in the area. Carefully avoiding any opportunity for my mediumistic friend to see that plaque, Horace Burr, Virginia Cloud, Ingrid, and I arrived at The Farm at three o'clock in the afternoon and immediately proceeded to the main room downstairs, where Ingrid stood transfixed in front of the colonial fireplace. To her, the little house looked like any other pre-colonial stone building; there was nothing to indicate that it had been of any significance in the past. As Ingrid stared at the fireplace, another strange thing happened. Almost simultaneously and frequently complementing one another, she and I got impressions from the past, rapidly, as it were; we both said whatever came to our minds. "I'm getting something about sickness in this room," Ingrid said, while I heard myself say, "I get the feeling of people with long rifles, shooting from the upper story. They are wearing gray jackets and light-colored pants, and the rifles are very long. This is in the direction away from the fireplace." Both of us said that men were making plans in the house at one time, and that it had to do with the defense of the building.

"I have the feeling that wounded people are being brought in right down here," Ingrid said. "I get the name Langdon or Langley and the name Nat." She walked around the room and then returned to her position near the fireplace. "I think the people with the light-colored breeches and the brown waistcoats and the long rifles are watching the road nearby for someone to come up that road. This is like a blockhouse, and there is some great anxiety about someone on his way up here. This is a last-ditch defense; there are perhaps five or six men, and they are militia men. I get the feeling of them lying on their stomachs upstairs with those huge rifles pointing with their long barrels and bayonets on top of them. The bullets are homemade, and it is the middle of the night. And then I get the feeling of a skirmish."

"It is like a flank," I said, feeling my way through an indefinite something in the air. "Someone is coming from the *wrong direction* to defend it. They should be coming this way, but they're coming the other way. They are coming up rather than down, and this is a terrible catastrophe for the defenders. I think if they get through, then it is all over."

I asked Virginia Cloud whether she had felt anything in the place. "I had a feeling of sickness here, as if it might be a hospital. I see Redcoats, Tories."

I turned to Horace Burr, asking him to comment on our observations. He seemed plainly delighted. "Well, I thought the most amazing thing that you said was this kind of replay of a group of armed forces, a flank, because there was a very interesting little maneuver that happened down the road, an attempt to cut off the main body of the armed forces coming here.

The attempt went awry, though. The American troops were entrenched along the road here, expecting the British to come *this* way. Unfortunately, they came the *other* way, so the British did take Charlottesville for one night. This is a very little known fact of history, and I'm sure you wouldn't have been aware of it. What you said was so interesting because it was one of those little events that are enormously important but did not become generally known because the stratagem didn't work."

"What about the defense outpost here and the men with their rifles upstairs? Do they make any sense?"

"Yes, indeed. From upstairs you could see where this flank should have been down the road, and so they probably were up there looking out for the oncoming troops."

"What about their dress?"

"Of course, they were all colonial, not professional soldiers."

"What about the name Nat?"

"This house was owned at the time by Nicholas Merriweather Lewis. He was a colonel and George Washington's aide. Nat was a colonial nickname for Nicholas."

"What about sick people in here?"

"This was an important center, and the owner's wife, Mary Walker Lewis, was well known for her interest in the public and public affairs. Her father owned Castle Hill. She and her husband were first cousins, both descended from the original Nicholas Merriweather, who had come here from Wales via Jamestown."

Why had Ingrid been so fascinated by the fireplace and the area immediately before it? Although she couldn't pinpoint it in so many words, she insisted that something terribly important had taken place in that very room. To be sure, no ghost had stayed behind in The Farm. But an indelible imprint of an important link with the past was indeed still alive in the atmosphere of the little house.

It was on June 14, 1781, that Colonel Banastre Tarleton, the British commander, had been seen by John Jouett, who then took his famous ride to warn Jefferson and the legislature of the approaching British. About that, anon. When Tarleton finally got to Charlottesville late the same day, proceeding along the old Kings Highway and destroying several wagonloads of Continental supplies on the way, he thwarted the carefully laid plans of the defenders of Charlottesville, two hundred men to whom the defense of the village had been entrusted. They had been planning an ambush in the gorge below Monticello. Captain John Marson, in command of the detachment, was disappointed, but there was nothing to be done. As Tarleton entered Charlottesville, he saw The Farm, with Mrs. Lewis standing at the door, far more curious than frightened. "I think maybe I'll stay here," Tarleton is quoted as saying, and decided to make The Farm his headquarters for the night. Mrs. Lewis had heard all sorts of stories about the handsome Tarleton. The Colonel was twenty-seven and very courteous. "Madam, you dwell in a little paradise," she quoted him in her diary.

Tarleton spent the night in front of the fireplace which had so attracted Ingrid, leaving the rest of the house to Mrs. Lewis, whose husband was away with the Continental Army. He spent the night wrapped in his greatcoat, in a chair which once stood in front of the fireplace but which was taken to Carrsgrove, the home of Horace Burr, several years ago.

It had been an unforgettable day, as Horace Burr put it, and the only night Tarleton spent in the area. Evidently the imprint of the expected but never realized ambush and the feelings of the men lying in wait for their feared foe had been left so strongly in the atmosphere of the house that Ingrid and, to some extent, I were able to tune in on it and reconstruct it.

What can one possibly say about Carrsgrove that the owners,

Horace and Helen Burr, direct descendants of Aaron Burr, have not said at one time or another, either in person or in print? Carrsgrove is their home, and they live in it happily and with great style. But it is more than just a home; it is a landmark of great importance, meticulously maintained by Burr and gradually turned into a personal museum. Where else can you find a Gainsborough, a Hogarth portrait of the young King George III, and dozens upon dozens of fine paintings and art works of the seventeenth and eighteenth centuries? Where else can you find a complete blend of antiquities and today's way of life, a little garden with a terra cotta statuette, and, above all, so many important pieces of furniture directly associated with the American Revolution? Not only is Professor Burr the foremost art authority in Albemarle County, as the area is now called, but he can tell you within a fraction of a second who was married to whom two hundred years ago, who their children were, and who they married in turn; his genealogical knowledge is absolutely fascinating, if not frightening. However, all those whose births Horace Burr knows so intimately are the right kind of people, from the Virginia horse country's point of view—the old families. The Randolphs, the Carrs, the Merriweathers, the Lewises, and last but certainly not least, the Burrs.

When I visited the house for the first time in 1964, I was already overwhelmed by its historical atmosphere. People have lived continuously on the spot where Carrsgrove now stands, but the stone house was erected in 1748 by a certain David Reese. This was fourteen years before an Act of Assembly established the town to be called Charlottesville, in honor of Princess Charlotte of Mecklenburg-Strelitz, the wife of the new king, George III. From the Reese family the house passed into the Maury family.

A rising young lieutenant of only twenty years of age by the name of James Monroe, who had been with General Washington at Trenton, visited the house many times during the early years of the Revolutionary War. It was here on April 21, 1779, that the citizens of Albemarle County signed their own "Declaration of Independence." In 1787 the house passed into the hands of Mr. and Mrs. Hudson Martin, probably the first citizens of Charlottesville, except for Thomas Jefferson and the leaders of the Revolutionary War. Martin was George Washington's nephew and Mrs. Martin the daughter of Colonel Nicholas Merriweather Lewis, owner of The Farm in town. Later the house attracted the attention of James Monroe's brother, Joseph Jones Monroe, who purchased it in 1797. Fortunately, James Dinsmore, the famous architect, was then at work at Monticello, the home of Thomas Jefferson, and he was persuaded to design the mantelpiece of the fireplace at Carrsgrove as well.

In 1799 James Monroe was elected governor of Virginia, and the following year he decided to buy Carrsgrove from his brother. For the next nine years Carrsgrove was the home of James Monroe, who was later to become President of the United States. His granite bust done from life now stands in the garden of Carrsgrove.

But Monroe was not the only great American who left his imprint in the atmosphere of Carrsgrove. In 1824, when Lafayette visited Charlottesville, a party was given in his honor at the house. During the War between the States, the infamous General George A. Custer made the house his headquarters, renaming it Piedmont, the name often given to that part of Virginia. Some alterations were made in 1896 by the then owner, Price Maury, who united the original stone house with two other buildings which were already standing in 1790. The Burrs acquired the house in 1955.

It had been decided to spend the late morning of our second day in Charlottesville at the Burr house, culminating in luncheon.

Naturally, Ingrid knew nothing whatsoever about the house, and during the television interview I gave to the crew from Richmond I made sure that she did not have a chance to speak to anyone about it. Horace Burr thought we should try the library first, since the downstairs front portion of the house was in the oldest section. He was curious to see what Ingrid might discover in the beautifully appointed library, which would have done any English manor house proud.

It was quiet all around us when we entered the library. As I did so, I felt a strange chill traveling down my spine for which there seemed to be no rational explanation. I had no foreknowledge of any ghostly manifestations in that part of the house, and to the best of my knowledge, the library was simply that. When I remarked upon it, Ingrid cut in to say that she too felt an unusual chill. "There is a lot of malice here, not toward anyone in this house, but there is a plan to *execute* someone."

I requested that she seat herself in a comfortable chair in the library and try for the semitrance state in which the deeper layers of consciousness might be contacted. After a few moments, Ingrid continued. "I think there are three men, and they are making plans to kill one person in an ambush. This has to do with politics, and we are somewhere in the 1730s or 1740s. *I can hear them talk around the fireplace.* The room is very tiny, not too much furniture in it. The floor is bare. I have a feeling they are killing this person unjustly."

I noticed how Horace Burr was hanging on every word coming from her lips. "Why do they want to kill him?" I asked.

"He is a landowner. It has something to do with importing. They have a private grudge against him."

"Where is this ambush to take place?"

"About five or six miles from here. They're going to shoot him on his way home."

"Do they succeed?"

"Yes."

"Are they ever found out?"

"No." She added that the body was later discovered; it was not a presence she felt, but an imprint from the past.

"What was the explanation given for his death?"

"They said it was a robbery."

"Is there anything else you can find out about this man or the plot?"

"The man is a tradesman, but he is also interested in political office. Like a representative or a seat in the government."

"Can you catch his name?"

"He belongs to a prominent family. Something beginning with A."

Since Ingrid indicated that she could not get any more about the room, I turned to Horace Burr for verification of the material we had just heard.

"I know the family this concerns," he replied, "and since I have the invoice of what was in the house at that time, I know she is correct about the furniture."

"What about this ambush?"

"The builder of this house, David Reese, died only three years after he had moved in. It was a sudden and seemingly unexplained death. Just what happened to this man and why he died after such a short time, all these things make you kind of wonder."

"What about his running for the Assembly?"

"Not to my knowledge. However, a somewhat later owner, Joseph Jones Monroe, did sit in the House of Burgesses."

We decided to go to the upper floor. Walking up the narrow staircase, Ingrid found her way directly to a small bedroom on the other side of the house. I had written about this room in 1965, but

Ingrid had no idea where she was or what the room meant to anyone. In addition to a beautiful sixteenth-century bed, there was a hand-carved wooden chair in a prominent position—so prominent, in fact, that Ingrid could not help but sit down in it. I asked Ingrid to tell us about any impressions she might have about the room or the chair. Immediately she said, "I sense a tragedy here, and I think it involves a child."

"Oh, God," Burr exclaimed involuntarily. "Please go on."

"I think that someone may have sat in this chair and watched a child die or that something awful happened. I think it was a boy not older than seven. A disease that couldn't be treated. A lingering death. Something awful, like scarlet fever or cholera."

"What happened to the mother?"

"I sense that it is a woman's presence here trying to hold on to the life of the young child. She is alone somehow. The child is all she has. I think this was her home."

"Do you feel her presence here too?"

"Yes, but I sense the child very strongly. I think this was a child's room. The woman does everything she can with doctors, but nothing can be done. The child is delirious for a long time."

Since I knew from my own recollections of Carrsgrove and from the look Horace Burr gave me while Ingrid was speaking that she had accurately retold the story of the haunting in the room, I decided to test her in relation to the chair in which she was sitting. I pointed out a similar chair on the other side of the room. Evidently, they were a pair, both extremely well carved and at least two hundred or two hundred fifty years old. Ingrid insisted that her feelings concerned not an imprint from the past but an actual presence, something we usually call a ghost. As she was speaking, we all noticed a chandelier move considerably of its own volition. Later, after we had completed the session, we tried unsuccessfully to cause it to move by walking up and down the stairs, walking around the room itself, or doing whatever we could to create vibrations. The chandelier remained immobile.

But Ingrid could not get anything further about the chair. Somehow the overwhelming presence of the woman and the child canceled out any less potent impressions the chair might have carried. I turned to Horace Burr and asked him, as usual, for comments.

"Ingrid was very close to the tragedy which occurred here," he began. "The woman was sitting in this chair, and three feet from it is the spot where she killed herself. It was about her child, which she thought was hopelessly sick. As you know, Hans, we heard her sobbing voice many years after her death and thus discovered the tragedy which had occurred here many years before. But these could not be the chairs she sat in; they came later. The area, however, is correct. Incidentally, these are the oldest documented man-made things in America; they came over from Wales, first to Jamestown, and then to this area. These are the chairs that used to be in The Farm, and in one of them General Banastre Tarleton spent the night wrapped in his cloak in 1781. Incidentally, the unfortunate woman whose presence Ingrid felt here took poison because she felt the child would be deformed. Her dying gasps were heard at the other end of the hall, across the stairwell into the master bedroom, where her father was sleeping, and as he stepped out into the hall and heard her gasps, she died. The child, however, grew up to be a perfectly normal and beautiful young woman."

Which proves that a powerful ghostly manifestation from this century can very well overcome the rambling, though pungent, thoughts of an eighteenth-century British general, especially if he, as Tarleton did, enjoyed the hospitality of his Revolutionary "enemies" far more than was customary under the circumstances.

3

Michie Tavern, Jefferson, and the Boys

"This typical pre-Revolutionary tavern was a favorite stopping place for travelers," the official guide to Charlottesville says. "With its colonial furniture and china, its beamed and paneled rooms, it appears much the way it did in the days when Jefferson and Monroe were visitors. Monroe writes of entertaining Lafayette as his guest at dinner here, and General Andrew Jackson, fresh from his victory at New Orleans, stopped over on his way to Washington."

The guide, however, does not mention that the tavern was moved a considerable distance from its original place to a much more accessible location where the tourist trade could benefit from it more. Regardless of this comparatively recent change of position, the tavern is exactly as it was, with everything inside, including its ghosts, intact. At the original site, it was surrounded by trees which framed it and sometimes towered over it. At the new site, facing the road, it looks out into the Virginia countryside almost like a manor house. One walks up to the wooden structure over a number of steps and enters the old tavern to the left or, if one prefers, the pub to the right, which is nowadays a coffee shop. Taverns in the eighteenth and early nineteenth centuries were not simply bars or inns; they were meeting places where people could talk freely, sometimes about political subjects. They were used as headquarters for Revolutionary movements or for invading military forces. Most taverns of any size had ballrooms in which the social functions of the area could be held. Only a few private individuals were wealthy enough to have their own ballrooms built into their manor houses.

What is fortunate about Michie Tavern is the fact that everything is pretty much as it was in the eighteenth century, and whatever restorations have been undertaken are completely authentic. The furniture and cooking utensils, the tools of the innkeeper, the porcelain, the china, the metal objects are all of the period, whether they had been in the house or not. As is customary with historical restorations or preservations, whatever is missing in the house is supplied by painstaking historical research, and objects of the same period and the same area are substituted for those presumably lost during the intervening period.

On my first visit to Charlottesville in 1964, Virginia Cloud had wanted me to visit the tavern, but somehow the schedule did not permit it then. This time the four of us arrived in mid-morning, in order to see the tavern before the tourists came—the luncheon crowd might make an interview with the current manager of the coffee shop difficult. The tavern has three floors and a large number of rooms, so we would need the two hours we had allowed ourselves for the visit. After looking at the downstairs part of the tavern, with its "common" kitchen and the over-long wooden table where two dozen people could be fed, we mounted the stairs to the second floor.

Ingrid kept looking into various rooms, sniffing out the psychic presences, as it were, while I followed close behind. Horace Burr and Virginia Cloud kept a respectable distance, as if trying not to "frighten" the ghosts away. That was all right with me, because I did not want Ingrid to tap the unconscious of either one of these very knowledgeable people.

Finally we arrived in the third-floor ballroom of the old tavern. I asked Ingrid what she had felt in the various rooms below. "In the pink room on the second floor I felt an argument or some sort of strife but nothing special in any of the other rooms."

"What about this big ballroom?"

"I can see a lot of people around here. There is a gay atmosphere, and I think important people came here; it is rather exclusive, this room. I think it was used just on special occasions."

By now I had waved Horace and Virginia to come closer, since it had become obvious to me that they wanted very much to hear what Ingrid was saying. Possibly new material might come to light, unknown to both of these historians, in which case they might verify it later on or comment upon it on the spot.

"I'm impressed with an argument over a woman here," Ingrid continued. "It has to do with one of the dignitaries, and it is about one of their wives."

"How does the argument end?"

"I think they just had a quick argument here, about her infidelity."

"Who are the people involved?"

"I think Hamilton. I don't know the woman's name."

"Who is the other man?"

"I think Jefferson was here."

"Try to get as much of the argument as you can."

Ingrid closed her eyes, sat down in a chair generally off limits to visitors, and tried to tune in on the past. "I get the argument as a real embarrassment," she began. "The woman is frail, she has a long dress on with lace at the top part around the neck, her hair is light brown."

"Does she take part in the argument?"

"Yes, she has to side with her husband."

"Describe her husband."

"I can't see his face, but he is dressed in a brocade jacket pulled back with buttons down the front and breeches. It is a very fancy outfit."

"How does it all end?"

"Well, nothing more is said. It is just a terrible embarrassment."

"Is this some sort of special occasion? Are there other people here?"

"Yes, oh, yes. It is like an anniversary or something of that sort. Perhaps a political anniversary of some kind. There is music and dancing and candlelight."

While Ingrid was speaking, in an almost inaudible voice, Horace and Virginia were straining to hear what she was saying but not being very successful at it. At this point Horace waved to me, and I tiptoed over to him. "Ask her to get the period a little closer," he whispered in my ear.

I went back to Ingrid and put the question to her. "I think it was toward the end of the war," she said, "toward the very end of it. For some time now I've had the figure 1781 impressed on my mind."

Since nothing further seemed to be forthcoming from Ingrid at this point, I asked her to relax and come back to the present, so that we could discuss her impressions freely.

"The name Hamilton is impossible in this connection," Horace Burr began. But I was quick to interject that the name Hamilton was fairly common in the late eighteenth and early nineteenth centuries and that Ingrid need not have referred to *the* Alexander Hamilton. "Jefferson was here many times, and he could have been involved in this," Burr continued. "I think I know who the other man might have been. But could we, just for once, try questioning the medium on specific issues?"

Neither Ingrid nor I objected, and Horace proceeded to ask Ingrid to identify the couple she had felt in the ballroom. Ingrid threw her head back for a moment, closed her eyes, and then replied, "The man is very prominent in politics, one of the big three or four at the time, and one of the reasons this is all so embarrassing, from what I get, is that the other man is of much lower caliber. He is not one of the big leaders; he may be an officer or something like that."

While Ingrid was speaking, slowly, as it were, I again felt the strange sense of transportation, of looking back in time, which had been coming to me more and more often recently, always unsought and usually only of fleeting duration. "For what it is worth," I said, "while Ingrid is speaking, I also get a very vague impression that all this has something to do with two sisters. It concerns a rivalry between two sisters."

"The man's outfit," Ingrid continued her narrative, "was sort of gold and white brocade and very fancy. He was the husband. I don't see the other man."

Horace seemed unusually agitated at this. "Tell me, did this couple live in this vicinity or did they come from far away on a special anniversary?"

"They lived in the vicinity and came just for the evening."

"Well, Horace?" I said, getting more and more curious, since he was apparently driving in a specific direction. "What was this all about?"

For once, Horace enjoyed being the center of attraction. "Well, it was a hot and heavy situation, all right. The couple were Mr. and Mrs. John Walker—he was the son of Dr. Walker of Castle Hill. And the man, who wasn't here, was Jefferson himself. Ingrid is right in saying that they lived in the vicinity—Castle Hill is not far away from here."

"But what about the special festivity that brought them all together here?"

Horace wasn't sure what it could have been, but Virginia, in great excitement, broke in here. "It was in this room that the waltz was danced for the first time in America. A young man had come from France dressed in very fancy clothes. The lady he danced with was a closely chaperoned girl from Charlottesville. She was very young, and she danced the waltz with this young man, and everybody in Charlottesville was shocked. The news went around town that the young lady had danced with a man holding her, and that was just terrible at the time. Perhaps that was the occasion. Michie Tavern was a stopover for stagecoaches, and Jefferson and the local people would meet here to get their news. Downstairs was the meeting room, but up here in the ballroom the more special events took place, such as the introduction of the waltz."

I turned to Horace Burr. "How is it that this tavern no longer stands on the original site? I understand it has been moved here for easier tourist access."

"Yes," Horace replied. "The building originally stood near the airport. In fact, the present airport is on part of the old estate that belonged to Colonel John Henry, the father of Patrick Henry. Young Patrick spent part of his boyhood there. Later, Colonel Henry sold the land to the Michies. This house was then their main house. It was on the old highway. In turn, they built themselves an elaborate mansion which is still standing and turned this house into a tavern. All the events we have been discussing took place while this building was on the old site. In 1926 it was moved here. Originally, I think the ballroom we are standing in now was just the loft of the old Henry house. They raised part of the roof to make it into a ballroom because they had no meeting room in the tavern."

In the attractively furnished coffee shop to the right of the main tavern, Mrs. Juanita Godfrey, the manager, served us steaming hot black coffee and sat down to chat with us. Had anyone ever complained about unusual noises or other inexplicable manifestations in the tavern? I asked.

"Some of the employees who work here at night do hear certain sounds they can't account for," Mrs. Godfrey replied. "They will hear something and go and look, and there will be nothing there."

"In what part of the building?"

"All over, even in this area. This is a section of the slave quarters, and it is very old."

Mrs. Godfrey did not seem too keen on psychic experiences, I felt. To the best of her knowledge, no one had had any unusual experiences in the tavern. "What about the lady who slept here one night?" I inquired.

"You mean Mrs. Milton—yes, she slept here one night." But Mrs. Godfrey knew nothing of Mrs. Milton's experiences.

However, Virginia had met the lady, who was connected with the historical preservation effort of the community. "One night when Mrs. Milton was out of town," Virginia explained, "I slept in her room. At the time she confessed to me that she had heard footsteps frequently, especially on the stairway down."

"That is the area she slept in, yes," Mrs. Godfrey confirmed. "She slept in the ladies' parlor on the first floor."

"What about yourself, Virginia? Did *you* hear anything?"

"I heard noises, but the wood sometimes behaves very funny. She, however, said they were definitely footsteps. That was in 1961."

What had Ingrid unearthed in the ballroom of Michie Tavern? Was it merely the lingering imprint of America's first waltz, scandalous to the early Americans but innocent in the light of today? Or was it something more—an involvement between Mrs. Walker and the illustrious Thomas Jefferson? My image of the great American had always been that of a man above human frailties. But my eyes were to be opened still further on a most intriguing visit to Monticello, Jefferson's home.

4

A Visit with the Spirited Jefferson

"You're welcome to visit Monticello to continue the parapsychological research which you are conducting relative to the personalities of 1776," wrote James A. Bear, Jr., of the Thomas Jefferson Memorial Foundation, and he arranged for us to go to the popular tourist attraction after regular hours, to permit Ingrid the peace and tranquility necessary to tune in on the very fragile vibrations that might hang on from the past.

Jefferson, along with Benjamin Franklin, has become a popular historical figure these days: a play, a musical, and a musical film have brought him to life, showing him as the shy, dedicated, intellectual architect of the Declaration of Independence. Jefferson, the gentle Virginia farmer, the man who wants to free the slaves but is thwarted in his efforts by other Southerners; Jefferson, the ardent but bashful lover of his wife; Jefferson, the ideal of virtue and American patriotism—these are the images put across by the entertainment media, by countless books, and by the tourist authorities which try to entice visitors to come to Charlottesville and visit Jefferson's home, Monticello.

Even the German tourist service plugged itself into the Jefferson boom. "This is like a second mother country for me," Thomas Jefferson is quoted as saying while traveling down the Rhine. "Everything that isn't English in our country comes from here." Jefferson compared the German Rhineland to certain portions of Maryland and Pennsylvania and pointed out that the second largest ethnic group in America at the time were Germans. In an article in the German language weekly *Aufbau*, Jefferson is described as the first prominent American tourist in the Rhineland. His visit took place in April 1788. At the time Jefferson was ambassador to Paris, and the Rhine journey allowed him to study agriculture, customs, and conditions on both sides of the Rhine. Unquestionably, Jefferson, along with Washington, Franklin, and Lincoln, represents one of the pillars of the American edifice.

Virginia Cloud, ever the avid historian of her area, points out that not only did Jefferson and John Adams have a close relationship as friends and political contemporaries but there were certain uncanny "coincidences" between their lives. For instance, both Jefferson and Adams died within hours of each other, Jefferson in Virginia and Adams in Massachusetts, on July 4, 1826—exactly fifty years to the day they had both signed the Declaration of Independence. Adams's last words were, "But Jefferson still lives." At the time that was no longer true, for Jefferson had died earlier in the day.

Jefferson's imprint is all over Charlottesville. Not only did the talented "Renaissance man" design his own home, Monticello, but he also designed the Rotunda, the focal point of the University of Virginia. Jefferson, Madison, and Monroe were members of the first governing board of the University, which is now famous for its school of medicine—and which, incidentally, is the leading university in the study of parapsychology, since Dr. Ian Stevenson teaches there.

On our way to Monticello we decided to visit the old Swan Tavern, which had some important links with Jefferson. The tavern is now used as a private club, but the directors graciously allowed us to come in, even the ladies, who are generally not admitted. Nothing in the appointments reminds one of the old tavern, since the place has been extensively remodeled to suit the requirements of the private club. At first we inspected the downstairs and smiled at several elderly gentlemen who hadn't the slightest idea why we were there. Then we went to the upper story and finally came to rest in a room to the rear of the building. As soon as Ingrid had seated herself in a comfortable chair in a corner, I closed the door and asked her what she felt about this place, of which she had no knowledge.

"I feel that people came here to talk things over in a lighter vein, perhaps over a few drinks."

"Was there anyone in particular who was outstanding among these people?"

"I keep thinking of Jefferson, and I'm seeing big mugs; most of the men have big mugs in front of them."

Considering that Ingrid did not know the past of the building as a tavern, this was pretty evidential. I asked her about Jefferson.

"I think he was the figurehead. This matter concerned him greatly, but I don't think it had anything to do with his own wealth or anything like that."

"At the time when this happened, was there a warlike action in progress?"

"Yes, I think it was on the outskirts of town. I have the feeling that somebody was trying to reach this place and that they were waiting for somebody, and yet they weren't really expecting that person."

Both Horace Burr and Virginia Cloud were visibly excited that Ingrid had put her finger on it, so to speak. Virginia had been championing the cause of the man about whom Ingrid had just spoken. "Virginians are always annoyed to hear about Paul Revere, who was actually an old man with a tired horse that left Revere to walk home," Virginia said, somewhat acidly, "while Jack Jouett did far more—he saved the lives of Thomas Jefferson and his legislators. Yet, outside of Virginia, few have ever heard of him."

"Perhaps Jouett didn't have as good a press agent as Paul Revere had in Longfellow, as you always say, Virginia," Burr commented. I asked Virginia to sum up the incident that Ingrid had touched on psychically.

"Jack Jouett was a native of Albemarle County and was of French Huguenot origin. His father, Captain John Jouett, owned this tavern."

"We think there is a chance that he also owned the Cuckoo Tavern in Louisa, forty miles from here," Burr interjected.

"Jouett had a son named Jack who stood six feet, four inches and weighed over two hundred pounds. He was an expert rider and one of those citizens who signed the oath of allegiance to the Commonwealth of Virginia in 1779.

"It was June 3, 1781, and the government had fled to Charlottesville from the advancing British troops. Most of Virginia was in British hands, and General Cornwallis very much wanted to capture the leaders of the Revolution, especially Thomas Jefferson, who had authored the Declaration of Independence, and Patrick Henry, whose motto, 'Give me liberty or give me death,' had so much contributed to the success of the

Revolution. In charge of 250 cavalrymen was Sir Banastre Tarleton. His mission was to get to Charlottesville as quickly as possible to capture the leaders of the uprising. Tarleton was determined to cover the seventy miles' distance between Cornwallis's headquarters and Charlottesville in a single twenty-four-hour period, in order to surprise the leaders of the American independence movement.

"In the town of Louisa, forty miles distant from Charlottesville, he and his men stopped into the Cuckoo Tavern for a brief respite. Fate would have it that Jack Jouett was at the tavern at that moment, looking after his father's business. It was a very hot day for June, and the men were thirsty. Despite Tarleton's orders, their tongues loosened, and Jack Jouett was able to overhear their destination. Jack decided to outride them and warn Charlottesville. It was about ten P.M. when he got on his best horse, determined to take short cuts and side roads, while the British would have to stick to the main road. Fortunately it was a moonlit night; otherwise he might not have made it in the rugged hill country.

"Meanwhile the British were moving ahead too, and around eleven o'clock they came to a halt on a plantation near Louisa. By two A.M. they had resumed their forward march. They paused again a few hours later to seize and burn a train of twelve wagons loaded with arms and clothing for the Continental troops in South Carolina. When dawn broke over Charlottesville, Jouett had left the British far behind. Arriving at Monticello, he dashed up to the front entrance to rouse Jefferson; however, Governor Jefferson, who was an early riser, had seen the rider tear up his driveway and met him at the door. Ever the gentleman, Jefferson offered the exhausted messenger a glass of wine before allowing him to proceed to Charlottesville proper, two miles farther on. There he roused the other members of the government, while Jefferson woke his family. Two hours later, when Tarleton came thundering into Charlottesville, the government of Virginia had vanished."

"That's quite a story, Virginia," I said.

"Of course," Burr added, "Tarleton and his men might have been here even earlier if it hadn't been for the fact that they first stopped at Castle Hill. Dr. and Mrs. Walker entertained them lavishly and served them a sumptuous breakfast. It was not only sumptuous but also delaying, and Dr. Walker played the perfect host to the hilt, showing Tarleton about the place despite the British commander's impatience, even to measuring Tarleton's orderly on the living-room door jamb. This trooper was the tallest man in the British army and proved to be six feet, nine and one-quarter inches in height. Due to these and other delaying tactics—and there are hints that Mrs. Walker used her not inconsiderable charms as well to delay the visitors—the Walkers made Jack Jouett's ride a complete success. Several members of the legislature who were visiting Dr. Walker at the time were captured, but Jefferson and the bulk of the legislature, which had just begun to convene early in the morning, got away.

"You see, the legislature of Virginia met in this building, and Ingrid was entirely correct with her impressions. The members of the legislature knew, of course, that the British were not far away, but they weren't exactly expecting them here."

After Thomas Jefferson had taken refuge at the house of a certain Mr. Cole, where he was not likely to be found, Jouett went to his room at his father's tavern, the very house we were in. He had well deserved his rest. Among those who were hiding from British arrest was Patrick Henry. He arrived at a certain farmhouse and identified himself by saying, "I'm Patrick Henry." But the farmer's wife replied, "Oh, you couldn't be, because my husband is out there fighting, and Patrick Henry would be out there too." Henry managed to convince the farmer's wife that his life depended on his hiding in her house, and finally she understood. But it was toward the end of the Revolutionary War and the British knew very well that they had for all intents and purposes been beaten. Consequently, shortly afterward, Cornwallis suggested to the Virginia legislators that they return to Charlottesville to resume their offices.

It was time to proceed to Monticello; the afternoon sun was setting, and we would be arriving just after the last tourists had left. Monticello, which every schoolboy knows from its representation on the American five-cent piece, is probably one of the finest examples of American architecture, designed by Jefferson himself, who lies buried here in the family graveyard. It stands on a hill looking down into the valley of Charlottesville, perhaps fifteen minutes from the town proper. Carefully landscaped grounds surround the house. Inside, the house is laid out in classical proportions. From the entrance hall with its famous clock, also designed by Jefferson, one enters a large, round room, the heart of the house. On both sides of this central area are rectangular rooms. To the left is a corner room, used as a study and library from where Jefferson, frequently early in the morning before anyone else was up, used to look out on the rolling hills of Virginia. Adjacent to it is a very small bedroom, almost a bunk. Thus, the entire west wing of the building is a self-contained apartment in which Jefferson could be active without interfering with the rest of his family. On the other side of the round central room is a large dining room leading to a terrace which, in turn, continues into an open walk with a magnificent view of the hillside. The furniture is Jefferson's own, as are the silver and china, some of it returned to Monticello in recent years by history-conscious citizens of the area who had purchased it in various ways.

The first room we visited was Jefferson's bedroom. Almost in awe herself, Ingrid touched the bedspread of what was once Thomas Jefferson's bed, then his desk and the books he had handled. "I feel his presence here," she said, "and I think he did a lot of his work in this room, a lot of planning and working things out, till the wee hours of the night." I don't think Ingrid knew that Jefferson was in the habit of doing just that, in this particular room.

I motioned Ingrid to sit down in one of Jefferson's chairs and try to capture whatever she might receive from the past. "I can see an awful lot of hard work, sleepless nights and turmoil. Other than that, nothing."

We went into the library next to the study. "I don't think he spent much time here really, just for reference." On we went to the dining room to the right of the round central room. "I think this was his favorite room, and he loved to meet people here socially." Then she added, "I get the words plum pudding and hot liquor."

"Well," Burr commented, "he loved the lighter things of life. He brought ice cream to America, and he squirted milk directly from the cow into a goblet to make it froth. He had a French palate. He liked what we used to call floating island, a very elaborate dessert."

"I see a lot of people. It is a friendly gathering with glittering glasses and candlelight," Ingrid said. "They are elegant but don't have on overcoats. I see their white silken shirts. I see them laughing and passing things around. Jefferson is at the table with white hair pulled back, leaning over and laughing."

The sun was setting, since it was getting toward half past six now, and we started to walk out the French glass doors onto the terrace. From there an open walk led around a sharp corner to a small building, perhaps twenty or twenty-five yards distant. Built

A Visit with the Spirited Jefferson [55]

in the same classical American style as Monticello itself, the building contained two fair-sized rooms, on two stories. The walk led to the entrance to the upper story, barricaded by an iron grillwork to keep tourists out. It allowed us to enter the room only partially, but sufficiently for Ingrid to get her bearings. Outside, the temperature sank rapidly as the evening approached. A wind had risen, and so it was pleasant to be inside the protective walls of the little house.

"Horace, where are we now?" I asked.

"We are in the honeymoon cottage where Thomas Jefferson brought his bride and lived at the time when his men were building Monticello. Jefferson and his family lived here at the very beginning, so you might say that whatever impressions there are here would be of the pre-Revolutionary part of Jefferson's life."

I turned to Ingrid and asked for her impressions. "I feel everything is very personal here and light, and I don't feel the tremendous strain in the planning of things I felt in the Monticello building. As I close my eyes, I get a funny feeling about a bouquet of flowers, some very strong and peculiar exotic flowers. They are either pink or light red and have a funny name, and I have the feeling that a woman involved in this impression is particularly fond of a specific kind of flower. He goes out of his way to get them for her, and I also get the feeling of a liking for a certain kind of chinaware or porcelain. Someone is a collector and wants to buy certain things, being a connoisseur, and wants to have little knick-knacks all over the place. I don't know if any of this makes any sense, but this is how I see it."

"It makes sense indeed," Horace Burr replied. "Jefferson did more to import rare trees and rare flowering shrubs than anyone else around here. In fact, he sent shipments back from France while he stayed there and indicated that they were so rare that if you planted them in one place they might not succeed. So he planted only a third at Monticello, a third at Verdant Lawn, which is an old estate belonging to a friend of his, and a third somewhere else in Virginia. It was his idea to plant them in three places to see if they would thrive in his Virginia."

"The name Rousseau comes to mind. Did he know anyone by that name?" Ingrid asked.

"Of course, he was much influenced by Rousseau."

"I also get the feeling of a flickering flame, a habit of staying up to all hours of the morning. Oh, and is there any historical record of an argument concerning this habit of his, between his wife and himself and some kind of peacemaking gesture on someone else's part?"

"I am sure there was an argument," Horace said, "but I doubt that there ever was a peacemaking gesture. You see, their marriage was not a blissful one; she was very wealthy and he spent her entire estate, just as he spent Dabney Carr's entire estate and George Short's entire estate. He went through estate after estate, including his own. Dabney Carr was his cousin, and he married Jefferson's sister, Martha. He was very wealthy, but Jefferson gathered up his sister and the children and brought them here after Carr's death. He then took over all the plantations and effects of Mr. Carr.

"Jefferson was a collector of things. He wrote three catalogues of his own collection, and when he died it was the largest collection in America. You are right about the porcelain, because it was terribly sophisticated at that time to be up on porcelain. The clipper trade was bringing in these rarities, and he liked to collect them."

Since Ingrid had scored so nicely up to now, I asked her whether she felt any particular emotional event connected with this little house.

"Well, I think the wife was not living on her level, her

standard, and she was unhappy. It wasn't what she was used to. It wasn't grand enough. I think she had doubts about him and his plans."

"In what sense?"

"I think she was dubious about what would happen. She was worried that he was getting too involved, and she didn't like his political affiliations too well."

I turned to Horace for comments. To my surprise, Horace asked me to turn off my tape recorder since the information was of a highly confidential nature. However, he pointed out that the material could be found in *American Heritage*, and that I was free to tell the story in my own words.

Apparently, there had always been a problem between Jefferson and his wife concerning other women. His associations were many and varied. Perhaps the most lasting was with a beautiful young black girl, about the same age as his wife. She was the illegitimate natural child of W. Skelton, a local gentleman, and served as a personal maid to Mrs. Jefferson. Eventually, Jefferson had a number of children by this girl. He even took her to Paris. He would send for her. This went on for a number of years and eventually contributed to the disillusionment of this girl. She died in a little room upstairs, and they took the coffin up there some way, but when they put it together and got her into the coffin, it wouldn't come downstairs. They had to take all the windows out and lower her on a rope. And what was she doing up there in the first place? All this did not contribute to Mrs. Jefferson's happiness. The irony is that, after Jefferson's death, two of his mulatto children were sent to New Orleans and *sold* as prostitutes to pay his debts. There are said to be some descendants of that liaison still alive today, but you won't find any of this in American textbooks.

Gossip and legend intermingle in small towns and in the

countryside. This is especially true when important historical figures are involved. So it is said that Jefferson did not die a natural death. Allegedly, he committed suicide by cutting his own throat. Toward the end of Jefferson's life, there was a bitter feud between himself and the Lewis family. Accusations and counteraccusations are said to have gone back and forth. Jefferson is said to have had Merriweather Lewis murdered and, prior to that, to have accused Mr. Lewis of a number of strange things that were not true. But none of these legends and rumors can be proved in terms of judicial procedure; when it comes to patriotic heroes of the American Revolution, the line between truth and fiction is always rather indistinct.

5

A Revolutionary Corollary: Patrick Henry, Nathan Hale, et al.

Nathan Hale, as every schoolboy knows, was the American spy hanged by the British. He was captured at Huntington Beach and taken to Brooklyn for trial. How he was captured is a matter of some concern to the people of Huntington, Long Island. The town was originally settled by colonists from Connecticut who were unhappy with the situation in that colony. There were five principal families who accounted for the early settlement of Huntington, and to this day their descendants are the most prominent families in the area. They were the Sammes, the Downings, the Busches, the Pauldings, and the Cooks. During the Revolutionary War, feelings were about equally divided among the town people: some were Revolutionaries and some remained Tories. The consensus of historians is that members of these five prominent families, all of whom were Tories, were responsible for the betrayal of Nathan Hale to the British.

All this was brought to my attention by Mrs. Geraldine P. of Huntington. Mrs. P. grew up in what she considers the oldest house in Huntington, although the Huntington Historical Society claims that theirs is even older. Be that as it may, it was there when the Revolutionary War started. Local legend has it that an act of violence took place on the corner of the street, which was then a crossroads in the middle of a rural area. The house in which Mrs. P. grew up stands on that street. Mrs. P. suspects that the capture—or, at any rate, the betrayal—of the Revolutionary agent took place on that crossroads. When she tried to investigate the history of her house, she found little cooperation on the part of the local historical society. It was a conspiracy of silence, according to her, as if some people wanted to cover up a certain situation from the past.

The house had had a "strange depressing effect on all its past residents," according to Mrs. P. Her own father, who studied astrology and white magic for many years, has related an incident that occurred several years ago in the house. He awoke in the middle of the night in the master bedroom because he felt unusually cold. He became aware of "something" rushing about the room in wild, frantic circles. Because of his outlook and training, he spoke up, saying, "Can I help you?" But the rushing about became even more frantic. He then asked what was wrong and what could be done. But no communication was possible. When he saw that he could not communicate with the entity, Mrs. P.'s father finally said, "If I can't help you, then go away." There was a snapping sound, and the room suddenly became quiet and warm again, and he went back to sleep. There have been no other recorded incidents at the house in question. But Mrs. P. wonders if some guilty entity wants to manifest, not necessarily

A Revolutionary Corollary

Nathan Hale, but perhaps someone connected with his betrayal.

At the corner of 43rd Street and Vanderbilt Avenue, Manhattan, one of the busiest and noisiest spots in all of New York City, there is a small commemorative plaque explaining that Nathan Hale, the Revolutionary spy, was executed on that spot by the British. I doubt that too many New Yorkers are aware of this, or can accurately pinpoint the location of the tragedy. It is even less likely that a foreigner would know about it. When I suggested to my good friend Sybil Leek that she accompany me to a psychically important spot for an experiment, she readily agreed. Despite the noises and the heavy traffic, the spot being across from Grand Central Station, Sybil bravely stood with me on the street corner and tried to get some sort of psychic impression.

"I get the impression of food and drink," Sybil said. I pointed out that there were restaurants all over the area, but Sybil shook her head. "No, I was thinking more of a place for food and drink, and I don't mean in the present. It is more like an inn, a transit place, and it has some connection with the river. A meeting place, perhaps, some sort of inn. Of course, it is very difficult in this noise and with all these new buildings here."

"If we took down these buildings, what would we see?"

"I think we would see a field and water. I have a strong feeling that there is a connection with water and with the inn. There are people coming and going—I sense a woman, but I don't think she's important. I am not sure . . . unless it would mean foreign. I hear a foreign language. Something like *Verchenen.** I can't quite get it. It is not German."

"Is there anything you feel about this spot?"

"This spot, yes. I think I want to go back two hundred years at least, it is not very clear, 1769 or 1796. That is the period. The connection with the water puzzles me."

---

* Verplanck's Point, on the Hudson River, was a Revolutionary strongpoint at the time.

"Do you feel an event of significance here at any time?"

"Yes. It is not strong enough to come through to me completely, but sufficiently *drastic* to make me feel a little nervous."

"In what way is it drastic?"

"Hurtful, violent. There are several people involved in this violence. Something connected with water, papers connected with water, that is part of the trouble."

Sybil then suggested that we go to the right to see if the impressions might be stronger at some distance. We went around the corner and I stopped. Was the impression any stronger?

"No, the impression is the same. Papers, violence. For a name, I have the impression of the letters P.T. Peter. It would be helpful to come here in the middle of the night, I think. I wish I could understand the connection with water, here in the middle of the city."

"Did someone die here?"

Sybil closed her eyes and thought it over for a moment. "Yes, but the death of this person was important at that time and indeed necessary. But there is more to it than just the death of the person. The disturbance involves lots of other things, lots of other people. In fact, two distinct races were involved, because I sense a lack of understanding. I think that this was a political thing, and the papers were important."

"Can you get anything further on the nature of this violence you feel here?"

"Just a disturbed feeling, an upheaval, a general disturbance. I am sorry I can't get much else. Perhaps if we came here at night, when things are quieter."

I suggested we get some tea in one of the nearby restaurants. Over tea, we discussed our little experiment and Sybil suddenly remembered an odd experience she had had when visiting the

Hotel Biltmore before. (The plaque in question is mounted on the wall of the hotel.) "I receive many invitations to go to this particular area of New York," Sybil explained, "and when I go I always get the feeling of repulsion to the extent where I may be on my way down and get into a telephone booth and call the people involved and say, 'No, I'll meet you somewhere else.' I don't like this particular area we just left; I find it very depressing. *I feel trapped.*"

I am indebted to R. M. Sandwich of Richmond, Virginia, for an intriguing account of an E.S.P. experience he has connected to Patrick Henry. Mr. Sandwich stated that he has had only one E.S.P. experience and that it took place in one of the early estate-homes of Patrick Henry. He admitted that the experience altered his previously dim view of E.S.P. The present owner of the estate has said that Mr. Sandwich has not been the only one to experience strange things in that house.

The estate-home where the incident took place is called Pine Flash and is presently owned by E. E. Verdon, a personal friend of Mr. Sandwich. It is located in Hanover County, about fifteen miles outside of Richmond. The house was given to Patrick Henry by his father-in-law. After Henry had lived in it for a number of years, it burned to the ground and was not rebuilt until fifteen years later. During that time Henry resided in the old cottage, which is directly behind the house, and stayed there until the main house had been rebuilt. This cottage is frequently referred to in the area as the honeymoon cottage of young Patrick Henry. The new house was rebuilt exactly as it had been before the fire. As for the cottage, which is still in excellent condition, it is thought to be the oldest wood frame dwelling in Virginia. It may have been there even before Patrick Henry lived in it.

On the Fourth of July, 1968, the Sandwiches had been invited to try their luck at fishing in a pond on Mr. Verdon's land. Since they would be arriving quite early in the morning, they were told that the oars to the rowboat, which they were to use at the pond, would be found inside the old cottage. They arrived at Pine Flash sometime around six A.M. Mrs. Sandwich started unpacking their fishing gear and food supplies, while Mr. Sandwich decided to inspect the cottage. Although he had been to the place several times before, he had never actually been inside the cottage itself.

Here then is Mr. Sandwich's report.

"I opened the door, walked in, and shut the door tight behind me. Barely a second had passed after I shut the door when a strange feeling sprang over me. It was the kind of feeling you would experience if you were to walk into an extremely cold, damp room. I remember how still everything was, and then I distinctly heard footsteps overhead in the attic. I called out, thinking perhaps there was someone upstairs. No one answered, nothing. At that time I was standing directly in front of an old fireplace. I admit I was scared half to death. The footsteps were louder now and seemed to be coming down the thin staircase toward me. As they passed me, I felt a cold, crisp, odd feeling. I started looking around for something, anything that could have caused all this. It was during this time that I noticed the closed door open very, very slowly. The door stopped when it was half opened, almost beckoning me to take my leave, which I did at great speed! As I went through that open door, I felt the same cold mass of air I had experienced before. Standing outside, I watched the door slam itself, almost in my face! My wife was still unpacking the car and claims she neither saw nor heard anything."

Revolutionary figures have a way of hanging on to places they like in life. Candy Bosselmann of Indiana has had a long history of psychic experiences. She is a budding trance medium and not at all ashamed of her talents. In 1964 she happened to be visiting Ashland, the home of Henry Clay, in Lexington, Kentucky. She had never been to Ashland, so she decided to take a look at it. She and other visitors were shown through the house by an older man, a professional guide, and Candy became somewhat restless listening to his historical ramblings. As the group entered the library and the guide explained the beautiful ash paneling taken from surrounding trees (for which the home is named), she became even more restless. She knew very well that it was the kind of feeling that forewarned her of some sort of psychic event. As she was looking over toward the fireplace, framed by two candelabra, she suddenly saw a very tall, white-haired man in a long black frock coat standing next to it. One elbow rested on the mantel, and his head was in his hand, as if he were pondering something very important.

Miss Bosselmann was not at all emotionally involved with the house. In fact, the guided tour bored her, and she would have preferred to be outside in the stables, since she has a great interest in horses. Her imagination did not conjure up what she saw: she knew in an instant that she was looking at the spirit imprint of Henry Clay.

In 1969 she visited Ashland again, and this time she went into the library deliberately. With her was a friend who wasn't at all psychic. Again, the same restless feeling came over her. But when she was about to go into trance, she decided to get out of the room in a hurry.

Rock Ford, the home of General Edward Hand, is located four miles south of Lancaster, Pennsylvania, and commands a fine view of the Conestoga River. The house is not a restoration but a well-preserved eighteenth-century mansion, with its original floors, railings, shutters, doors, cupboards, panelings, and window glass. Even the original wall painting can be seen. It is a four-story brick mansion in the Georgian style, with the rooms grouped around a center hall in the design popular during the latter part of the eighteenth century. The rooms are furnished with antiquities of the period, thanks to the discovery of an inventory of General Hand's estate which permitted the local historical society to supply authentic articles of daily usage wherever the originals had disappeared from the house.

Perhaps General Edward Hand is not as well known as a hero of the American Revolution as others are, but to the people of the Pennsylvania Dutch country he is an important figure, even though he was of Irish origin rather than German. Trained as a medical doctor at Trinity College, Dublin, he came to America in 1767 with the Eighteenth Royal Irish Regiment of Foote. However, he resigned British service in 1774 and came to Lancaster to practice medicine and surgery. With the fierce love of liberty so many of the Irish possess, Dr. Hand joined the Revolutionaries in July of 1775, becoming a lieutenant colonel in the Pennsylvania Rifle Battalion. He served in the army until 1800, when he was discharged as a major general. Dr. Hand was present at the Battle of Trenton, the Battle of Long Island, the Battle of White Plains, the Battle of Princeton, the campaign against the Iroquois, and the surrender of Cornwallis at Yorktown. He also served on the tribunal which convicted Major John André, the British spy, and later became the army's adjutant general. He was highly regarded by George Washington, who visited him in his home toward the end of the war. When peace came, Hand became a member of the Continental Congress and served in the Assembly of Pennsylvania as representative of his area. He moved into Rock Ford when it was completed in 1793 and died there in September 1802.

A Revolutionary Corollary

Today, hostesses from a local historical society serve as guides for the tourists who come to Rock Ford in increasing numbers. Visitors are taken about the lower floor and basement and are told of General Hand's agricultural experiments, his medical studies, and his association with George Washington. But unless you ask specifically, you are not likely to hear about what happened to the house after General Hand died. To begin with, the General's son committed suicide in the house. Before long the family died out, and eventually the house became a museum since no one wanted to live in it for very long. At one time, immigrants were contacted at the docks and offered free housing if they would live in the mansion. None stayed. There was something about the house that was not as it should be, something that made people fear it and leave it just as quickly as they could.

Mrs. Ruth S. lives in upstate New York. In 1967 a friend showed her a brochure concerning Rock Ford, and the house intrigued her. Since she was traveling in that direction, she decided to pay Rock Ford a visit. With her family, she drove up to the house and parked her car in the rear. At that moment she had an eerie feeling that something wasn't right. Mind you, Mrs. S. had not been to the house before, had no knowledge about it nor any indication that anything unusual had occurred in it. The group of visitors was quite small. In addition to herself and her family, there were two young college boys and one other couple. Even though it was a sunny day, Mrs. S. felt icy cold.

"I felt a presence before we entered the house and before we heard the story from the guide," she explained. "If I were a hostess there, I wouldn't stay there alone for two consecutive minutes." Mrs. S. had been to many old houses and restorations before but had never felt as she did at Rock Ford.

It is not surprising that George Washington should be the

subject of a number of psychic accounts. Probably the best known (and most frequently misinterpreted) story concerns General Washington's vision which came to him during the encampment at Valley Forge, when the fortunes of war had gone heavily in favor of the British, and the American army, tattered and badly fed, was just about falling to pieces. If there ever was need for divine guidance, it was at Valley Forge. Washington was in the habit of meditating in the woods at times and saying his prayers when he was quite alone. On one of those occasions he returned to his quarters more worried than usual. As he busied himself with his papers, he had the feeling of a presence in the room. Looking up, he saw opposite him a singularly beautiful woman. Since he had given orders not to be disturbed, he couldn't understand how she had gotten into the room. Although he questioned her several times, the visitor would not reply. As he looked at the apparition, for that is what it was, the General became more and more entranced with her, unable to make any move. For a while he thought he was dying, for he imagined that the apparition of such unworldly creatures as he was seeing at that moment must accompany the moment of transition.

Finally, he heard a voice, saying, "Son of the Republic, look and learn." At the same time, the visitor extended her arm toward the east, and Washington saw what to him appeared like white vapor at some distance. As the vapor dissipated, he saw the various countries of the world and the oceans that separated them. He then noticed a dark, shadowy angel standing between Europe and America, taking water out of the ocean and sprinkling it over America with one hand and over Europe with the other. When he did this, a cloud rose from the countries thus sprinkled, and the cloud then moved westward until it enveloped America. Sharp flashes of lightning became visible at intervals in the cloud. At the same time, Washington thought he heard the anguished cries of the American people underneath the cloud. Next, the strange visitor showed him a vision of what America would look like in the future, and he saw villages and towns springing up from one coast to the other until the entire land was covered by them.

"Son of the Republic, the end of the century cometh, look and learn," the visitor said. Again Washington was shown a dark cloud approaching America, and he saw the American people fighting one another. A bright angel then appeared wearing a crown on which was written the word Union. This angel bore the American Flag, which he placed between the divided nation, saying, "Remember, you are brethren." At that instant, the inhabitants threw away their weapons and became friends again.

Once more the mysterious voice spoke. "Son of the Republic, look and learn." Now the dark angel put a trumpet to his mouth and sounded three distinct blasts. Then he took water from the ocean and sprinkled it on Europe, Asia, and Africa. As he did so, Washington saw black clouds rise from the countries he had sprinkled. Through the black clouds, Washington could see red light and hordes of armed men, marching by land and sailing by sea to America, and he saw these armies devastate the entire country, burn the villages, towns, and cities, and as he listened to the thundering of the cannon, Washington heard the mysterious voice saying again, "Son of the Republic, look and learn."

Once more the dark angel put the trumpet to his mouth and sounded a long and fearful blast. As he did so, a light as of a thousand suns shone down from above him and pierced the dark cloud which had enveloped America. At the same time the angel wearing the word Union on his head descended from the heavens, followed by legions of white spirits. Together with the inhabitants of America, Washington saw them renew the battle and heard the mysterious voice telling him, once again, "Son of the Republic, look and learn."

For the last time, the dark angel dipped water from the ocean and sprinkled it on America; the dark cloud rolled back and left the inhabitants of America victorious. But the vision continued. Once again Washington saw villages, towns, and cities spring up, and he heard the bright angel exclaim, "While the stars remain and the heavens send down dew upon the earth, so long shall the Union last." With that, the scene faded, and Washington beheld once again the mysterious visitor before him. As if she had guessed his question, the apparition then said:

"Son of the Republic, what you have seen is thus interpreted: Three great perils will come upon the Republic. The most fearful is the third, during which the whole world united shall not prevail against her. Let every child of the Republic learn to live for his God, his land, and his Union." With that, the vision disappeared, and Washington was left pondering over his experience.

One can interpret this story in many ways, of course. If it really occurred, and there are a number of accounts of it in existence which lead me believe that there is a basis of fact to this, then we are dealing with a case of prophecy on the part of General Washington. It is a moot question whether the third peril has already come upon us, in the shape of World War II, or whether it is yet to befall us. The light that is stronger than many suns may have ominous meaning in this age of nuclear warfare.

Washington himself is said to have appeared to Senator Calhoun of South Carolina at the beginning of the War between the States. At that time, the question of secession had not been fully decided, and Calhoun, one of the most powerful politicians in the government, was not sure whether he could support the withdrawal of his state from the Union. The question lay heavily on his mind when he went to bed one hot night in Charleston, South Carolina. During the night, he thought he awoke to see the apparition of General George Washington standing by his bedside. The General wore his presidential attire and seemed surrounded by a bright outline, as if some powerful source of light shone behind him. On the senator's desk lay the declaration of secession, which he had not yet signed. With Calhoun's and South Carolina's support, the Confederacy would be well on its way, having closed ranks. Earnestly, the spirit of George Washington pleaded with Senator Calhoun not to sign the declaration. He warned him against the impending perils coming to America as a divided nation; he asked him to reconsider his decision and to work for the preservation of the Union. But Calhoun insisted that the South had to go its own way. When the spirit of Washington saw that nothing could sway Senator Calhoun, he warned him that the very act of his signature would be a black spot upon the Constitution of the United States. With that, the vision is said to have vanished.

One can easily explain the experience as a dream, coming as it did at a time when Senator Calhoun was particularly upset over the implications of his actions. On the other hand, there is this to consider: Shortly after Calhoun had signed the document taking South Carolina into the Confederacy, a dark spot appeared on his hand, a spot that would not vanish and for which medical authorities had no adequate explanation.

Mrs. Margaret Smith of Orlando, Florida, has had a long history of psychic experiences. She has personally seen the ghostly monks of Beaulieu, England; she has seen the actual lantern of Joe Baldwin, the famous headless ghost of Wilmington, North Carolina; and she takes her "supernatural" experiences in her stride the way other people feel about their musical talents or hobbies. When she was only a young girl, her grandmother took her to visit the von Steuben house in Hackensack, New Jersey. (General F. W. A. von Steuben was a German supporter of the

American Revolution who aided General Washington with volunteers who had come over from Europe because of repressions, hoping to find greater freedom in the New World.) The house was old and dusty, the floorboards were creaking, and there was an eerie atmosphere about it. The house had been turned into an historical museum, and there were hostesses to take visitors through.

While her grandmother was chatting with the guide downstairs, the young girl walked up the stairs by herself. In one of the upstairs parlors she saw a man sitting in a chair in the corner. She assumed he was another guide. When she turned around to ask him a question about the room, he was gone. Since she hadn't heard him leave, that seemed rather odd to her, especially as the floorboards would creak with every step. But being young she didn't pay too much attention to this peculiarity. A moment later, however, he reappeared. As soon as she saw him, she asked the question she had on her mind. This time he did not disappear but answered her in a slow, painstaking voice that seemed to come from far away. When he had satisfied her curiosity about the room, he asked her some questions about herself, and finally asked the one which stuck in her mind for many years afterward—"What is General Washington doing now about the British?"

Margaret was taken aback at this question. She was young, but she knew very well that Washington had been dead for many years. Tactfully, she told him this and added that Harry Truman was now president and that the year was 1951. At this information, the man looked stunned and sat down again in the chair. As Margaret watched him in fascinated horror, he faded away.

6

The Philipsburg Manor Ghost

The Philipses were Dutch Americans of immense wealth and prestige, early settlers along the Hudson River who built manor houses and castles as if they were still in Europe. Their wealth came primarily from two sources—agriculture, especially the milling of grain, and fisheries. Mining, especially for building materials, had not yet developed to any significant size in the area when the Philipses were in their heyday. As can be expected from such a well-established and well-entrenched family, they were arch-conservative and supported the kinds of causes that were most likely to sustain them and give them additional wealth. Later on, when the Revolutionary War cut through so many family ties, there were exceptions to this, and sometimes the cause of freedom won out over the cause of money.

When I first made inquiries about Philipse Manor, I was

confused by the reference to it as Philipse Castle until I realized that I was talking about the same thing. The village was called Philipsborough and in colonial days was designated a manor, that is, a principal house surrounded by a few farmers' houses. The castle itself stands on the Pocantico River, which, according to Harry Hansen, author of *North of Manhattan*, "flows out from between dark, tree-bordered hills and, gaining momentum, winds past the southwest boundary of Sleepy Hollow Cemetery and under the modern Headless Horseman Bridge. There it reaches the wide millpond and gathers weight to push the millwheel below the dam. Glancing back at the modern motor age, we observed that the road is U.S. 9, the locality North Tarrytown."

I visited Philipsburg Manor in the company of Ingrid Beckman and two interested friends from Long Island who had agreed to drive us there in return for visiting a house owned by them. We almost missed the place. We were looking for a sign saying Philipse Castle, or at least Philipsburg Manor; instead, we came upon one that read Upper Mills. Thinking that the handsome colonial building in front of us was merely the lower part of the establishment, and that there was a larger, even more impressive building somewhere farther back, we kept circling the millhouse several times until we realized that we had arrived after all.

Mill and castle stand side by side, meticulously restored to the way they were in colonial days. Even the guides are costumed in eighteenth-century attire, a touch that must go down well with the tourists from, say, Detroit or Omaha. The mill itself is so well restored that it actually grinds corn, and you can see the wooden machinery in operation. Since this is a private project dependent on income from tourism and gifts, the grain thus milled is sold and, I understand, is of superior quality to the commercial product.

Over a short wooden bridge one reaches the manor house

proper. An artificial dam faithful to eighteenth-century models has been reconstructed—so well, in fact, that it actually works the mill better than electrical power could. One can stand on the wooden footbridge and see the water gather momentum, then be channeled into wooden troughs that feed the large wooden wheel of the mill and thus set the milling machinery inside in motion.

The castle itself is a large two-story house with a gambrel roof, and two immense square chimneys protruding from it. Fully restored from ugly, later additions, it now looks exactly the way it did in the mid-eighteenth century. With the help of Rockefeller money, the castle stands "as an example of the well-to-do American household," as Hansen put it. In colonial times, when most farm buildings were made of wood, this stone house was referred to as Philipse-his-Castle, and that is how the name has carried over into today. After the Philipse family, being of Tory persuasion, had departed for England at the close of the Revolutionary War, the manor was acquired by Gerard Beekman, who erected a wooden addition to it in 1785. The original stone house had only two rooms on the ground floor and two bedrooms above them, but this soon proved inadequate, and so an annex was added containing another two rooms each on the two floors and an additional chimney. Apparently the annex was added while the first part was still being built, for the roof shows evidence of having been built all at one time.

Harry Hansen suggests that the house be viewed in candlelight, so that the furniture of the period can be appreciated as it was when the house was new. He also suggests that one enter it by the basement door and work one's way up. This we did, observing first the food stores and the slave quarters, for the early Dutch settlers had plenty of involuntary help who attended the open hearth where they ate their meals. During Indian alarms, livestock was sheltered in these quarters, thus emphasizing the relative position of slaves and animals. As the house was well supplied with food stores, and solidly built, it could endure very long sieges, if necessary, and perhaps that, too, accounts for the castle designation. There is even a row of narrow ports overlooking the harbor which were intended for guns. The harbor itself was closer to the house than it is now, the river having deposited silt and mud during the past two centuries which now form the land on which a very ugly modern gasoline refinery stands. One gazes upon colonial Philipse Manor to the right; then, turning in a thirty-degree angle, one beholds this modern monstrosity. Not very good area planning, frankly, but that is the way it is in our country.

During the years of restoration, hundreds of fragments of eighteenth-century pottery were recovered from the grounds and the millpond and are now on exhibit in the lower part of the manor. One must remember that ships were able to come quite close to the house, practically within sight of it, and so goods could be loaded from and unloaded to the house directly. There are fragments of broken wine glasses that may have been used to toast the King of England, since the owners of this house were solidly pro-British, despite their Dutch origins.

The first floor contains the family dining room, while next to it is an office once used by the overseer of the establishment. The front room, now furnished as a social room, would have been the parlor during the Philipse tenancy. There is a large stone fireplace with blue Delft plates for decorations. Finally, there is another parlor, larger than the first one, containing much fine early American furniture and the oldest known painting of New Amsterdam. There was no formal staircase in this house as is so often found in early colonial houses. Instead, two narrow sets of stairs, strictly functional, lead to the upper stories.

The second floor contains four bedrooms. The two to the west

The Philipsburg Manor Ghost

are slightly lower than those in the east, further evidence that the house was built in two sections. The eastern wing contains a smaller children's room and the master bedroom. The central piece of furniture here is an impressive four-poster bed, covered with embroidered fabrics and a painted coverlet made around 1700, said to have come from the East Indies and showing the tree-of-life motif.

Finally there is the attic, where the slaves slept or worked at various crafts, such as the carding of wool, weaving, and spinning. The roof itself is new, but most of the original rafters are still there. Part of the attic is the Beekman addition, and the staircase leads down to the second floor of that section of the house. At a time when the Philipses were either dead or had fled to England, the house was seized by the committee on forfeiture of the State of New York, along with 750 acres of the plantation. It was sold to a patriotic, pro-Revolutionary family, the Beekmans, in 1785. The original document testifying to that transaction for the sum of 9,040 pounds, with the signatures of Isaac Stoutenburgh and Philip van Cortlandt, commissioners, may be seen in one of the rooms. The change was a political one for the house, not one of social or even national background, for the Beekmans were also Dutch-Americans and of the same landed gentry class as the Philipses had been. If the Philipses hadn't backed the wrong side in the Revolutionary War, this never would have happened. They were on intimate terms with the Beekmans and the van Cortlandts; in fact, the families intermarried frequently. But because of the bitterness at the close of the Revolutionary War, houses and possessions of families who had actively supported the British were bound to be seized as the property of traitors.

With the help of Miss Pat Smith, librarian for the restorations, we were able to inspect the premises leisurely and with a minimum of interference from tourists. Ingrid had never been to this place and knew nothing about it. After inspecting the lower portion, we walked up the stairs to the second floor. Suddenly Ingrid reported a feeling of heaviness as she went up the stairs. We entered the east wing, and Ingrid stopped in front of the four-poster bed in the master bedroom. "I think it has something to do with this bed," she said. "It feels almost like suffocation. *Something has happened here.*" With that, Ingrid touched the bed, the wood, the cover, and then stepped back again.

"If you care to try it," the curator said, inviting Ingrid to lie down on the bed.

Ingrid shook her head. She touched it again. "I feel a great heaviness around this area."

"Try to close your eyes and visualize whatever might have happened in this bed," I requested.

"You know," Ingrid said instead, "I meant to tell you at the parking lot that when you said this was the Upper Mills, I knew it wasn't the right place. I felt that *this* house was the place we were looking for all along. At the time I felt, well, if this *isn't* the house we're looking for, then it has something in it of a psychic nature as well."

"What did you feel when we were still out there?"

"I felt a female presence."

"Now that we are in the bedroom, what do you feel about it?"

"I think there is something violent here. I think someone suffered and died here. This is the room I felt all along."

I suggested we walk around the room and that Ingrid touch various objects in it as well as the walls in order to see if there were any particular areas more strongly affected by whatever was hanging on from the past.

"For some strange reason, I feel particularly attracted to that chair, or at least the area of the chair," she said. Since the room was furnished with a table, four chairs, and a chest of drawers, and graced by a fireplace across from the bed, picking out one particular chair was at least interesting. "I have this strong feeling about the area where the bed stands. It is hard to believe what you feel when you put your head in there," she said, placing her head underneath the canopy. Suddenly she withdrew it.

"What's the matter?" I asked, knowing from her expression that she had heard or seen something.

"I heard a little noise."

"What sort of noise?"

"It sounded like a tapping."

None of the others had heard anything, but then they didn't possess Ingrid's psychic powers. "Try to visualize what might have transpired in this place," I suggested.

Ingrid looked at me with a terrified expression in her eyes. "I think a woman was murdered here."

"Details, please."

"I think she was in her thirties or forties. This happened a long time ago, in the late 1700s. I think a man did it, and he may have been related to her in some way. I think she was caught unawares."

"What was the motive?"

"I think it was jealousy. Perhaps money was involved, too, but jealousy, definitely, and the murderer may have been a relative, someone who knew her."

"Can you tell me more about her?"

"She was a married woman, there were children, and I got the name Sarah. I'm sorry, but I can't get the family name just now."

"Is this a presence in the true sense or merely an imprint from the past?"

"It might be just an imprint, for it doesn't seem to be heavy enough to be a presence, but it is something that I am reliving right now."

"Can you describe her physically?"

"I think she might be tallish and a little slight, between thirty and forty years of age, dressed in long clothes, a loose skirt, sort of red, perhaps rose, and a white blouse or smock."

"How was she murdered?"

"I think she was strangled. I see a man with black hair, younger than she was, and I don't think there was anyone in the house when this happened."

"Did he get away with it?"

"Yes. He runs from the scene. When he strangled her, she fell back onto the bed, and that is where she was found. I don't know whether he strangled her in bed, but I'm sure she was found *here*."

"Who found her?"

"Her husband, and possibly the children."

Since Ingrid had no idea what Philipse Manor stood for, or who the people were who built it and lived here, I felt safe in asking the next question. "Do you have any idea what sort of work the people did here?"

"I think there was a lot of farming involved. Maybe he was a tradesman of some sort in town. What he traded he got here, or something of that sort."

"Do you get any feeling of political or warlike action around here?"

"There is an air of general turbulence around this entire area. There may have been some jealousy concerning the husband's business, or his land, or something of that kind, which caused this man to murder the woman."

Since Ingrid had apparently exhausted her impressions of this room, I suggested that we try some of the other rooms to see whether anything might be hanging on in them from the past. "Down those steps," Ingrid said, and pointed at the stairs. "I think he came down the front staircase when he got away. He got out the back door."

We walked Ingrid all over the house, from room to room, passageway to passageway, staircase one and staircase two. In each area she "sniffed" psychically and reported nothing out of the ordinary. Finally I decided to return to the master bedroom, where Ingrid had gotten such a strong impression. "Now that we are back here in the upper bedroom, what do you feel?"

"Again, as I come in, I have a tingling feeling up my spine. It is dangerous in here. I had this feeling as I came up the stairs before and looked into the room."

I thought that she might approach the story fresh and perhaps get additional information. This time Ingrid decided to lie down on the bed, but she did so as if she were lying on burning coals, always ready to jump up. She closed her eyes but was fully conscious. "I guess the husband's assets had a lot to do with the crime."

"Do you get his name?"

"Thomas. The fellow who murdered her is a very stocky man, rather short, with black hair. I get the name Michael."

"Can you tell me whether he is a military man or a civilian? Is he from here or is he from somewhere else?"

"I think he is from this area and knows the family or is related to them. He is involved in some sort of conspiracy, some organization. Still, I keep getting jealousy, and that he is involved in some large movement. It is political as well as personal, I mean the jealousy. Her husband is quite important to this entire area. He may even be involved in the government in town. I also think her husband is away when it happens."

Since we had been all over the house, including the attic, and Ingrid had not received any further impressions, I thought it was time to discuss what we had just heard and see whether any of it might be proven. As had been happening with increasing frequency lately, I myself was receiving certain slight impressions about the place and thought it best to communicate them to the others, for what the impressions might be worth. For instance, while Ingrid was looking at the four-poster in the haunted bedroom, I distinctly felt that the name George was very important, and I had the fleeting impression of someone in a red uniform of sorts. This was either an officer or a military person with the cavalry, and I had the feeling that something had to be delivered to this house because it was important to a group of people who were waiting for word of something. I also had the feeling, which came to me when we first entered the house, that some meetings had taken place not in that room but downstairs. These, I thought, were meetings and discussions on a very high level and of a quasi-political nature. Something had been started here and was later continued somewhere else. I also thought that this was not a generally known fact, and I was not at all sure that it could be checked out.

I then turned to Mr. and Mrs. C. Mack, the young couple who had brought us here in their car and who had both had a number of psychic experiences in their own house in the country. Had they had any impressions while we were going through the house? "Just a stumbling feeling in the bedroom and the initials A.S., and then something also on the stairway going down," Mrs. Greta Mack said.

"What kind of feeling?" I said, for I hadn't quite understood.

"A very stumbling feeling, as if I were going to fall."

I then turned to Pat Smith and asked her about her own impressions. Miss Smith pointed out that Philipsburg Manor was heavily restored and that most of the furniture had been brought in from other areas, although of the same period.

By itself, this would make psychometry more difficult, except that I thought Ingrid was "reading" the immediate area of the house rather than the physical furniture. Most of the authentic Philipse material, consisting of broken bits of porcelain and clay pipes, lay neatly arranged in dozens of boxes in the attic, where the interview with Miss Smith took place. Yet Ingrid received no psychic impression while we were up in the attic.

"Miss Smith," I asked, "did the Philipses deal in goods, that is to say, were they tradesmen as Ingrid intimated?"

"Yes, indeed. Frederick Philipse brought himself up from being basically Governor Stuyvesant's carpenter to the fourth richest merchant in the area."

"Were they politically active during the Revolution?"

"Yes, they were," Pat Smith replied. "I recall your mentioning an impression of a red jacket. I'd like to comment on this. Adolph Philipse was the last one of the family who really cared to run this place as a mercantile business. The restoration itself cuts off with 1750, which is the year of his death. But there was another Frederick, the second of his name, who was a Tory. He was imprisoned in Westchester and eventually was released but lost his property under the forfeiture act and died in Cheshire, England."

I knew what she was driving at. British officers wore red jackets. So did some of their sympathizers. "Were there ever any political meetings in this house?"

"I don't know for sure, but I do know that Frederick Philipse, while in a Yankee prison, wrote to his wife to please send him a lemon with one of their slaves since he was afraid of getting scurvy. But in truth, he wasn't worried about getting scurvy; he was much more worried about secret messages, and in one letter he observed, 'Please tell the children to be very careful what they say.' His children were eleven and twelve and had been partially responsible for getting him into prison, by speaking out too frankly. He would put nothing but innocuous expressions into his letters. His secret messages he is said to have hidden in the fold of the envelope."

"What sort of a man was this Philipse?"

"I understand he was a very fat man—in fact, his wife wouldn't ride in the same carriage with him, and she complained that he drove too fast. As far as meetings in this house are concerned, you know they wouldn't exactly publicize them at the time."

Suddenly, I remembered something else that had struck me while we were visiting the upstairs part of the house. At that time I had the distinct impression that a minister or pastor was involved with the family as a principal figure in some way.

"Well, I wouldn't be surprised," Miss Smith said. "They founded the Old Dutch Church across the street from here. This is the famous Old Dutch Church in the Legend of Sleepy Hollow. The Philipses are all buried there. At one time some archaeologists wanted to open the crypt and exhume some of these people in order to look at them, but the church would not let them. I have no idea what they were looking for."

Miss Smith herself never experienced anything out of the ordinary at the manor. She considers herself slightly interested in the occult, and has, in fact, had an experience at nearby Sunnyside, the home of Washington Irving. But then she never slept in the four-poster in the master bedroom either.

"The manor lords north of Manhattan had a gay and spirited social life in the eighteenth century in spite of the difficult travel over rocks and hills and the long distances between estates," comments Harry Hansen. "In winter they sent their families to New York, where their houses were within walking distance of the Battery."

Which one of the Philipse ladies died in this four-poster? It would seem to me that the absence, by force, of the lord of the manor would have been the most likely time for an outsider to get into the house and do his deed. Perhaps some courageous tourist visiting Philipse Manor on future occasions will lie down on the four-poster and get the rest of the story. In the meantime, the Philipsburg Manor ghost is a fading memory and won't scare the tourists away.

7

Major André and the Question of Loyalty

"Major John André's fateful excursion from General Sir Henry Clinton's headquarters at Number 1 Broadway to the gallows on the hill at Tappan took less than a week of the eighteenth century, exactly one hundred seventy years ago at this writing. It seems incredible that this journey should make memorable the roads he followed, the houses he entered, the roadside wells where he stopped to quench his thirst, the words he spoke. But it did." This eloquent statement by Harry Hansen goes a long way in describing the relative importance of so temporary a matter as the fate and capture of a British agent during the Revolutionary War.

In the Tarrytowns, up in Westchester County, places associated with André are considered prime tourist attractions. More research effort has been expended on the exploration of even the most minute detail of the ill-fated André's last voyage than on

Major André and the Question of Loyalty

some far worthier (but less romantic) historical projects elsewhere. A number of good books have been written about the incident, every schoolboy knows about it, and John André has gone into history as a gentlemanly but losing hero of the American Revolutionary War. But in presenting history to schoolchildren as well as to the average adult, most American texts ignore the basic situation as it then existed.

To begin with, the American Revolutionary War was more of a civil war than a war between two nations. Independence was by no means desired by all Americans; in fact, the Declaration of Independence had difficulty passing the Continental Congress and did so only after much negotiating behind the scenes and the elimination of a number of passages, such as those relating to the issue of slavery, considered unacceptable by Southerners. When the Declaration of Independence did become the law of the land—at least as far as its advocates were concerned—there were still those who had not supported it originally and who felt themselves put in the peculiar position of being disloyal to their new country or becoming disloyal to the country they felt they ought to be loyal to. Those who preferred continued ties with Great Britain were called Tories, and numbered among them generally were the more influential and wealthier elements in the colonies. There were exceptions, of course, but on the whole the conservatives did not support the cause of the Revolution by any means. Any notion that the country arose *as a man* to fight the terrible British is pure political make-believe. The issues were deep and manifold, but they might have been resolved eventually through negotiations. There is no telling what might have happened if both England and the United Colonies had continued to negotiate for a better relationship. The recent civil war in Spain was far more a war between two distinct groups than was the American Revolutionary War. In the latter, friends and enemies lived side by side in many areas, the lines were indistinctly drawn, and members of the same family might support one side or the other. The issue was not between Britain, the invading enemy, and America, the attacked; on the contrary, it was between the renunciation of all ties with the motherland and continued adherence to some form of relationship. Thus, it had become a political issue far more than a purely patriotic or national issue. After all, there were people of the same national background on both sides, and nearly everyone had relatives in England.

Under the circumstances, the question of what constituted loyalty was a tricky one. To the British, the colonies were in rebellion and thus disloyal to the king. To the Americans, anyone supporting the British government after the Declaration of Independence was considered disloyal. But the percentage of those who could not support independence was very large all through the war, far more than a few scattered individuals. While some of these Tories continued to support Britain for personal or commercial reasons, others did so out of honest political conviction. To them, helping a British soldier did not constitute high treason but, to the contrary, was their normal duty. Added to this dilemma was the fact that there were numerous cases of individuals crossing the lines on both sides, for local business reasons, to remove women and children caught behind the lines, or to parley about military matters, such as the surrender of small detachments incapable of rejoining their regiments, or the obtaining of help for wounded soldiers. The Revolutionary War was not savagely fought; it was, after all, a war between gentlemen. There were no atrocities, no concentration camps, and no slaughter of the innocent.

In the fall of 1780 the situation had deteriorated to a standstill of sorts, albeit to the detriment of the American forces. The British were in control of the entire South, and they held New

Major André and the Question of Loyalty

York firmly in their grip. The British sloop *Vulture* was anchored in the middle of the Hudson River opposite Croton Point. In this position, it was not too far from that formidable bastion of the American defense system, West Point. Only West Point and its multiple fortifications stood in the way of total defeat for the American forces.

Picture, if you will, the situation in and around New York. The British Army was in full control of the city, that is to say, Manhattan, with the British lines going right through Westchester County. The Americans were entrenched on the New Jersey shore and on both sides of the Hudson River from Westchester County upward. On the American side were first of all, the regular Continental Army, commanded by General Washington, and also various units of local militia. Uniforms for the militia men ran the gamut of paramilitary to civilian, and their training and backgrounds were also extremely spotty. It would have been difficult at times to distinguish a soldier of the Revolutionary forces from a civilian.

The British didn't call on the citizens of the area they occupied for special services, but it lay in the nature of this peculiar war that many volunteered to help either side. The same situation which existed among the civilian population in the occupied areas also prevailed where the Revolution was successful. Tory families kept on giving support to the British, and when they were found out they were charged with high treason. Nevertheless, they continued right on supplying aid. Moreover, the lines between British and American forces were not always clearly drawn. They shifted from day to day, and if anyone wanted to cross from north of Westchester into New Jersey, for instance, he might very well find himself in the wrong part of the country if he didn't know his way around or if he hadn't checked the latest information. To make matters even more confusing, Sir Henry Clinton was in charge of the British troops in New York City, while Governor Clinton ruled the state of New York, one of the thirteen colonies, from Albany.

In the spring of 1779 Sir Henry Clinton received letters from an unknown correspondent who signed himself only "Gustavus." From the content of these letters, the British commander knew instantly that he was dealing with a high-ranking American officer. Someone on the American side wished to make contact in order to serve the British cause. Clinton turned the matter over to his capable adjutant general, Major John André. André, whose specialty was what we call intelligence today, replied to the letters, using the pseudonym John Anderson.

André had originally been active in the business world but purchased a commission as a second lieutenant in the British Army in 1771. He arrived in America in 1774 and served in the Philadelphia area. Eventually he served in a number of campaigns and by 1777 had been promoted to captain. Among the wealthy Tory families he became friendly with during the British occupation of Philadelphia was the Shippen family. One of the daughters of that family later married General Benedict Arnold.

André's first major intelligence job was to make contact with a secret body of Royalists living near Chesapeake Bay. This group of Royalists had agreed to rise against the Americans if military protection were sent to them. Essentially, André was a staff officer, not too familiar with field work and therefore apt to get into difficulties once faced with the realities of rugged terrain. As the correspondence continued, both Clinton and André suspected that the Loyalist writing the letters was none other than General Benedict Arnold, and eventually Arnold conceded this.

After many false starts, a meeting took place between Major General Benedict Arnold, the commander of West Point, and

Major John André on the night of September 21, 1780, at Haverstraw on the Hudson. At the time, Arnold made his headquarters at the house of Colonel Beverley Robinson, which was near West Point.

The trip had been undertaken on André's insistence, very much against the wishes of his immediate superior, Sir Henry Clinton. As André was leaving, Clinton reminded him that under no circumstances was he to change his uniform or to take papers with him. It was quite sufficient to exchange views with General Arnold and then to return to the safety of the British lines.

Unfortunately, André disobeyed these commands. General Arnold had with him six papers which he persuaded André to place between his stockings and his feet. The six papers contained vital information about the fortifications at West Point, sufficient to allow the British to capture the strongpoint with Arnold's help. "The six papers which Arnold persuaded André to place between his stockings and his feet did not contain anything of value that could not have been entrusted to André's memory or at most contained in a few lines in cipher that would not have been intelligible to anyone else," states Otto Hufeland in his book *Westchester County during the American Revolution*. But it is thought that André still distrusted General Arnold and wanted something in the latter's handwriting that would incriminate him if there was any deception.

It was already morning when the two men parted. General Arnold returned to his headquarters by barge, leaving André with Joshua Smith, who was to see to his safe return. André's original plan was to get to the sloop *Vulture* and return to New York by that route. But somehow Joshua Smith convinced him that he should go by land. He also persuaded André to put on a civilian coat, which he supplied. General Arnold had given them passes to get through the lines, so toward sunset André, Smith, and a servant rode down to King's Ferry, crossing the river from Stony Point to Verplanck's Point and on into Westchester County.

Taking various back roads and little-used paths which made the journey much longer, André eventually arrived at a spot not far from Philipse Castle. There he ran into three militia men: John Paulding, Isaac Van Wart, and David Williams. They were uneducated men in their early twenties, and far from experienced in such matters as how to question a suspected spy. The three fellows weren't looking for spies, however, but for cattle thieves which were then plaguing the area. They were on the lookout near the Albany Post Road when Van Wart saw André pass on his horse. They stopped him, and that is where André made his first mistake. Misinterpreting the Hessian coat Paulding wore (he had obtained it four days before when escaping from a New York prison) and thinking that he was among British Loyalists, he immediately identified himself as a British officer and asked them not to detain him. But the three militia men made him dismount and undress, and then the documents were discovered. It has been said that they weren't suspicious of him at all, but that the elegant boots, something very valuable in those days, tempted them, and that they were more interested in André's clothing than in what he might have on him. Whatever the motivation, André was brought to Colonel Jameson's headquarters at Sand's Mill, which is called Armonk today.

Jameson sent the prisoner to General Arnold, a strange decision which indicates some sort of private motive. The papers, however, he sent directly to General Washington, who was then at Hartford. Only upon the return of his next-in-command, Major Tallmadge, did the real state of affairs come to light. On Tallmadge's insistence, the party escorting André to General Arnold was recalled and brought back to Sand's Mills. But a letter telling General Arnold of André's capture was permitted to continue on its way to West Point!

Benedict Arnold received the letter the next morning at breakfast. The General rose from the table, announced that he had to go across the river to West Point immediately, and went to his room in great agitation. His wife followed him, and he informed her that he must leave at once, perhaps forever. Then he mounted his horse and dashed down to the riverside. Jumping into his barge, he ordered his men to row him to the *Vulture*, some seventeen miles below. He explained to his men that he came on a flag of truce and promised them an extra ration of rum if they made it particularly quickly. When the barge arrived at the British vessel, he jumped aboard and even tried to force the bargemen to enter the King's service on the threat of making them prisoners. The men refused, and the *Vulture* sailed on to New York City. On arrival, General Clinton freed the bargemen, a most unusual act of gallantry in those days.

Meanwhile André was being tried as a spy. Found guilty by a court-martial at Tappan, he was executed by hanging on October 2, 1780. The three militia men who had thus saved the very existence of the new republic were voted special medals by Congress.

The entire area around Tappan and the Tarrytowns is "André" country. At Philipse Castle there is a special exhibit of André memorabilia in a tiny closet under the stairs. There is a persistent rumor that André was trying to escape from his captors. According to Mrs. Cornelia Beekman, who then lived at the van Cortlandt House in Peekskill, there was in her house a suitcase containing an American army uniform and a lot of cash. That suitcase was to be turned over to anyone bringing a written note from André. Joshua Hett Smith, who had helped André escape after his meeting with Arnold, later asked for the suitcase; however, as Smith had nothing in writing, Beekman refused to give it to him. However, this story came to light only many years after the Revolution, perhaps because Mrs. Beekman feared to be drawn into a treason trial or because she had some feelings of her own in the matter.

Our next stop was to be the van Cortlandt mansion, not more than fifteen minutes away by car. Obviously, Pat Smith was in a good mood this morning. In her little foreign car she preceded us at such a pace that we had great difficulty keeping up with her. It was a sight to behold how this lady eased her way in and out of traffic with an almost serpentine agility that made us wonder how long she could keep it up. Bravely following her, we passed Sleepy Hollow Cemetery and gave it some thought. No, we were not too much concerned with all the illustrious Dutch Americans buried there, nor with Washington Irving and nearby Sunnyside; we were frankly concerned with ourselves. Would we also wind up at Sleepy Hollow Cemetery, or would we make it to the van Cortlandt mansion in one piece . . . ?

The mansion itself is a handsome two-story building, meticulously restored and furnished with furniture and artworks of the eighteenth century, some of it from the original house. Turned into a tourist attraction by the same foundation which looked after Philipsburg Manor, the house, situated on a bluff, is a perfect example of how to run an outdoor museum. Prior to climbing the hill to the mansion itself, however, we visited the ferryboat house at the foot of the hill. In the eighteenth century and the early part of the nineteenth century, the river came close to the house, and it was possible for the ships bringing goods to the van Cortlandts to come a considerable distance inland to discharge their merchandise. The Ferryboat Inn seemed a natural outgrowth of having a ferry at that spot: the ferry itself crossed an arm of the Hudson

River, not very wide, but wide enough not to be forded on foot or by a small boat. Since so much of these buildings had been restored, I wondered whether Ingrid would pick up anything from the past.

The inn turned out to be a charming little house. Downstairs we found what must have been the public room, a kitchen, and another room, with a winding staircase leading to the upper story. Frankly, I expected very little from this but did not want to offend Pat Smith, who had suggested the visit.

"Funny," Ingrid said, "when I walked into the door, I had the feeling that I had to force my way *through a crowd.*"

The curator seemed surprised at this, for she hadn't expected anything from this particular visit either. "I can't understand this," she said plaintively. "This is one of the friendliest buildings we have."

"Well," I said, "ferryboat inns in the old days weren't exactly like the Hilton."

"I feel a lot of activity here," Ingrid said. "Something happened here, not a hanging, but connected with one."

We went upstairs, where I stopped Ingrid in front of a niche that contained a contemporary print of André's execution. As yet we had not discussed Major André or his connection with the area, and I doubt very much whether Ingrid realized there was a connection. "As you look at this, do you have any idea who it is?" I asked.

Ingrid, who is very nearsighted, looked at the picture from a distance and said, "I feel that he may have come through this place at one time." And so he might have.

As we walked up the hill to the van Cortlandt mansion, the time being just right for a visit as the tourists would be leaving, I questioned Pat Smith about the mansion.

"My mother used to know the family who owns the house,"

Pat Smith began. "Among the last descendants of the van Cortlandts were Mrs. Jean Brown and a Mrs. Mason. This was in the late thirties or the forties, when I lived in New Canaan. Apparently there were such manifestations at the house that the two ladies called the Archbishop of New York for help. They complained that a spirit was 'acting up,' that there were the sound of a coach that no one could see and other inexplicable noises of the usual poltergeist nature."

"What did they do about it?"

"Despite his reluctance to get involved, the Archbishop did go up to the manor, partly because of the prominence of the family. He put on his full regalia and went through a ritual of exorcism. Whether or not it did any good, I don't know, but a little later a psychic sensitive went through the house also and recorded some of these noises. As far as I know, none of it was ever published, and for all I know, it may still be there—the specter, that is."

We now had arrived at the mansion, and we entered the downstairs portion of the house. Two young ladies dressed in colonial costumes received us and offered us some cornmeal tidbits baked in the colonial manner. We went over the house from top to bottom, from bottom to top, but Ingrid felt absolutely nothing out of the ordinary. True, she felt the vibrations of people having lived in the house, having come and gone, but no tragedy, no deep imprint, and, above all, no presence. Pat Smith seemed a little disappointed. She didn't really *believe* in ghosts as such, but, having had some E.S.P. experiences at Sunnyside, she wasn't altogether sure. At that instant she remembered having left her shopping bag at the Ferryboat Inn. The bag contained much literature on the various colonial houses in the area, and she wanted to give it to us. Excusing herself, she dashed madly back down the hill to the Ferryboat Inn. She was back in no time, a little out of breath, which made me wonder whether she had wanted to make her solo visit to the Ferryboat Inn at dusk just as *brief* as humanly possible.

In a splendid Victorian mansion surmounted by a central tower, the Historical Society of the Tarrytowns functions as an extremely well organized local museum as well as a research center. Too prudent to display items of general interest that might be found elsewhere in greater quantity and better quality, the Historical Society concentrates on items and information pertaining to the immediate area. It is particularly strong on pamphlets, papers, maps, and other literature of the area from 1786 onward. One of the principal rooms in the Society's museum is the so-called Captors' Room. In it are displays of a sizable collection of material dealing with the capture of Major André. These include lithographs, engravings, documentary material, letters, and, among other things, a chair. It is the chair André sat in when he was still a free man at the Underhill home, south of Yorktown Heights. Mrs. Adelaide Smith, the curator, was exceptionally helpful to us when we stated the purpose of our visit. Again, as I always do, I prevented Ingrid from hearing my conversation with Mrs. Smith, or with Miss Smith, who had come along now that she had recovered her shopping bag full of literature. As soon as I could get a moment alone with Ingrid, I asked her to touch the chair in question.

"I get just a slight impression," she said, seating herself in the chair, then getting up again. "There may have been a meeting in here of some kind, or he may have been sentenced while near or sitting in this chair. I think there was a meeting in this room to determine what would happen."

But she could not get anything very strong about the chair.

Looking at the memorabilia, she then commented, "I feel he was chased for quite a while before he was captured. I do feel that the chair in this room has something to do with his sentence."

"Is the chair authentic?"

"Yes, I think so."

"Now concerning this room, the Captors' Room, do you feel anything special about it?"

"Yes, I think this is where it was decided, and I feel there were a lot of men here, men from town and from the government."

Had Ingrid wanted to manufacture a likely story to please me, she could not have done worse. Everything about the room and the building would have told her that it was of the nineteenth century, and that the impression she had just described seemed out of place, historically speaking. But those were her feelings, and as a good sensitive she felt obliged to say whatever came into her mind or whatever she was impressed with, not to examine it as to whether it fit in with the situation she found herself in. I turned to the curator and asked, "Mrs. Smith, what was this room used for, and how old is the building itself?"

"The building is about one hundred twenty-five years old; our records show it was built between 1848 and 1850 by Captain Jacob Odell, the first mayor of Tarrytown. It was built as one house, and since its erection two families have lived here. First, there were the Odells, and later Mr. and Mrs. Aussie Case. Mrs. Case is eighty-seven now and retired. This house was purchased for the Society to become their headquarters. It has been used as our headquarters for over twenty years."

"Was there anything on this spot before this house was built?"

"I don't know."

"Has anyone ever been tried or judged in this room?"

"I don't know."

Realizing that a piece of furniture might bring with itself part of the atmosphere in which it stood when some particularly emotional event took place, I questioned Mrs. Smith about the history of the chair.

"This chair, dated 1725, was presented to us from Yorktown. It was the chair in which Major André sat the morning of his capture, when he and Joshua Smith stopped at the home of Isaac Underhill for breakfast."

The thoughts going through André's head that morning, when he was almost sure of a successful mission, must have been fairly happy ones. He had succeeded in obtaining the papers from General Arnold; he had slept reasonably well, been fed a good breakfast, and was now, presumably, on his way to Manhattan and a reunion with his commanding general, Sir Henry Clinton. If Ingrid felt any meetings around that chair, she might be reaching back beyond André's short use of the chair, perhaps into the history of the Underhill home itself. Why, then, did she speak of sentence and capture, facts she would know from the well-known historical account of Major André's mission? I think that the many documents and memorabilia stored in the comparatively small room might have created a common atmosphere in which bits and snatches of past happenings had been reproduced in some fashion. Perhaps Ingrid was able to tune in on this shallow but nevertheless still extant psychic layer.

Major André became a sort of celebrity in his own time. His stature as a British master spy was exaggerated far out of proportion even during the Revolutionary War. This is understandable when one realizes how close the cause of American independence had come to total defeat. If André had delivered the documents entrusted to him by Major General Arnold to the British, West Point could not have been held. With the fall of the complicated fortifications at the point, the entire North would have soon been occupied by the British. Unquestionably, the capture of Major André was a turning point in the war, which had then reached a stalemate, albeit one in favor of the British. They could afford to wait and sit it out while the Continental troops were starving to death, unable to last another winter.

General Arnold's betrayal was by no means a sudden decision; his feelings about the war had changed some time prior to the actual act. The reasons may be seen in his background, his strong Tory leanings, and a certain resentment against the command of the Revolutionary Army. He felt he had not advanced quickly enough; the command at West Point was given him only three months prior to André's capture. Rather than being grateful for the belated recognition of his talents by the Continental command, Arnold saw it as a godsend to fulfill his own nefarious task. For several months he had been in correspondence with Sir Henry Clinton in New York, and his decision to betray the cause of independence was made long before he became commander of West Point.

But André wasn't the master spy later accounts try to make him out: his bumbling response when captured by the three militia men shows that he was far from experienced in such matters. Since he had carried on his person a *laissez-passer* signed by General Arnold, he needed only to produce this document and the men would have let him go. Instead, he *volunteered* the information that he was a British officer. All this because one of the militia men wore a Hessian coat. It never occurred to André that the coat might have been stolen or picked up on the battlefield! But there was a certain weakness in André's character, a certain conceit, and the opportunity of presenting himself as a British officer on important business was too much to pass up when he met the three nondescript militia men. Perhaps his personal vanity played a part in this fateful decision; perhaps he really believed himself to be among troops on his own side. Whatever the cause of his strange behavior, he paid with his life for it. Within weeks after the hanging of Major André, the entire Continental Army knew of the event, the British command was made aware of it, and in a detailed document Sir Henry Clinton explained what he had had in mind in case Arnold would have been able to deliver West Point and its garrison to the British. Thus, the name André became a household word among the troops of both sides.

In 1951 I investigated a case of a haunting at the colonial house belonging to the late *New York News* columnist Danton Walker. The case was first published, under the title "The Rockland County Ghost," in *Tomorrow* magazine and, later, in *Ghost Hunter*. Various disturbances had occurred at the house between 1941 and 1951 that had led Mr. Walker to believe that he had a poltergeist in his domicile. The late Eileen Garrett offered to serve as medium in the investigation, and Dr. Robert Laidlaw, the eminent psychiatrist, was to meet us at the house to supervise the proceedings along with me. Even before Mrs. Garrett set foot in the house, however, she revealed to us the result of a "traveling clairvoyance" expedition in which she had seen the entity "hung up" in the house. His name, she informed us, was Andreas, and she felt that he was attached to the then owner of the house.

The visit to the house was one of the most dramatic and perhaps traumatic psychic investigations into haunted houses I have ever conducted. The house, which has since changed ownership owing to Mr. Walker's death, stands on a hill that was once part of a large farm. During the Revolutionary War, the house served as headquarters for a detachment of troops on the Revolutionary side. General Anthony Wayne, known as "Mad Anthony," had his headquarters very near this site, and the Battle of Stony Point was fought just a few miles away in 1779. The building served as a fortified roadhouse used for the storage of arms, ammunitions, food, and at times for the safekeeping of prisoners.

At the time Danton Walker had bought the house, it was in a sad state of disrepair, but with patience and much money he restored it to its former appearance. During the time when the house was being rebuilt, Walker stayed at a nearby inn but would occasionally take afternoon naps on an army cot in the upstairs part of his house. On these occasions he had the distinct impression of the presence of a Revolutionary soldier in the same room with him. Psychic impressions were nothing new for the late *News* columnist; he had lived with them all his life. During the first two years of his tenancy, Walker did not observe anything further, but by 1944 there had developed audible and even visible phenomena.

One afternoon, while resting in the front room downstairs, he heard a violent knocking at the front door caused by someone moving the heavy iron knocker. But he found no one at the front door. Others, including Walker's man Johnny, were aroused many times by knocking at the door, only to find no one there. A workman engaged in the restoration of the house complained about hearing someone with heavy boots on walking up the stairs in mid-afternoon, at a time when he was alone in the place. The sound of heavy footfalls, of someone, probably male, wearing boots, kept recurring. During the summer of 1952, when Walker had guests downstairs, everyone heard the heavy thumping sound of someone falling down the stairs. Other, more tangible phenomena added to the eerie atmosphere of the place: the unmistakable imprint of a heavy man's thumb on a thick pewter jar of the seventeenth century, inexplicable on any grounds; the mysterious appearance on a plate rail eight feet above the kitchen floor of a piece of glass that had been in the front-door window; pictures tumbling down from their places in the hallway; and a pewter pitcher thrown at a woman guest from a bookshelf behind the bed.

One evening, two Broadway friends of Danton Walker's, both of them interested in the occult but not really believers, came to the house for the weekend. One of the men, L., a famous Broadway writer, insisted on spending the night in the haunted bedroom upstairs. An hour later the pajama-clad guest came down to Walker's little studio at the other end of the estate, where Walker was now sleeping because of the disturbances, and demanded an end to the "silly pranks" he thought someone was playing on him. The light beside his bed was blinking on and off, while all the other lights in the house were burning steadily, he explained. Walker sent him back to bed with an explanation about erratic power supply in the country. A little over an hour later, L. came running back to Walker and asked to spend the rest of the night in Walker's studio.

In the morning he explained the reasons for his strange behavior: he had been awakened from deep sleep by the sensation of someone slapping him violently about the face. Sitting bolt upright in bed, he noticed that the shirt he had placed on the back of a rocking chair was being agitated by the breeze. The chair was rocking ever so gently. It then occurred to L. that there could be no breeze in the room, since all the windows had been closed!

Many times, Walker had the impression that someone was trying *desperately* to get into the house, as if for refuge. He recalled that the children of a previous tenant had spoken of some disturbance near a lilac bush at the corner of the house. The original crude stone walk from the road to the house passed by this lilac bush and went on to the well, which, according to local tradition, had been used by Revolutionary soldiers.

Our group of investigators reached the house on November 22, 1952, on a particularly dark day, as if it had been staged that way.

Toward three o'clock in the afternoon, we sat down for a séance in the upstairs bedroom. Within a matter of seconds, Eileen Garrett had disappeared, so to speak, from her body, and in her stead was another person. Sitting upright and speaking in halting tones with a distinct oriental accent, Uvani, one of Mrs. Garrett's spirit guides, addressed us and prepared us for the personality that would follow him.

"I am confronted myself with a rather restless personality, a very strange personality, and one that might appear to be, in his own life, perhaps not quite of the right mind," he explained to us. The control personality then added that he was having difficulty maintaining a calm atmosphere owing to the great disturbance the entity was bringing into the house. As the control spoke, the medium's hands and legs began to shake. He explained that she was experiencing the physical condition of the entity that would soon speak to us, a disease known as classical palsy. Dr. Laidlaw nodded and asked the entity to proceed.

A moment later, the body of Eileen Garrett was occupied by an entirely new personality. Shaking uncontrollably, as if in great pain, the entity tried to sit up in the chair but was unable to maintain balance and eventually crashed to the floor. There, one of the legs continued to vibrate violently, which is one of the symptoms of palsy, a disease in which muscular control is lost. For two minutes or more, only inarticulate sounds came from the entranced medium's lips. Eventually we were able to induce the possessing entity to speak to us. At first there were only halting sounds, as if the entity were in great pain. From time to time the entity touched his leg, and then his head, indicating that those were areas in which he experienced pain. Dr. Laidlaw assured the personality before us that we had come as friends and that he could speak with us freely and without fear. Realizing what we were attempting to convey, the entity broke into tears, extremely agitated, and at the same time trying to come close to where Dr. Laidlaw sat.

We could at last understand most of the words. The entity spoke English, but with a marked Polish accent. The voice sounded rough, uncouth, not at all like Eileen Garrett's own.

"Friend . . . friend . . . mercy. I know . . . I know . . . ," and he pointed in the direction of Danton Walker. As we pried, gently and patiently, more information came from the entity on the floor before us. "Stones, stones. . . . Don't let them take me. I can't talk." With that he pointed to his head, then to his tongue.

"No stones. You will not be stoned," Dr. Laidlaw assured him.

"No beatin'?"

Laidlaw assured the entity that he *could* talk, and that we were friends. He then asked what the entity's name might be.

"He calls me. I have to get out. I cannot go any further. In God's name, I cannot go any further."

With that, the entity touched Danton Walker's hands. Walker was visibly moved. "I will protect you," he said simply.

The entity kept talking about "stones," and we assumed that he was talking about stones being thrown at him. Actually, he was talking about stones under which he had hidden some documents. But that came later. Meanwhile he pointed at his mouth and said, "Teeth gone," and he graphically demonstrated how they had been kicked in. "Protect me," the entity said, coming closer to Walker again. Dr. Laidlaw asked whether he lived here. A violent gesture was his answer. "No, oh, no. I hide here. Cannot leave here."

It appeared that he was hiding from another man and that he knew the plans, which he had hidden in a faraway spot. "Where did you hide the plans?" Walker demanded.

"Give me map," the entity replied, and when Walker handed him a writing pad and a pen, the entity, using Mrs. Garrett's fingers, of course, picked it up as if he were handling a quill. The drawing, despite its unsteady and vacillating lines due to palsy, was nevertheless a valid representation of where the entity had hidden the papers. "In your measure, Andreas hid . . . not in the house . . . timber house, log house . . . under the stones . . . fifteen stones . . . plans for the whole shifting of men and ammunitions I have for the French. Plans I have to deliver to log house, right where the sun strikes window. Where sun strikes the window . . . fifteen stones under in log house . . . there I have put away plans."

This was followed by a renewed outburst of fear, during which the entity begged us not to allow him to be taken again. After much questioning, the entity told us that he was in need of protection, that he was Polish and had come to this country as a young man. He threw his arms around Walker, saying that he was like a brother to him. "Gospodin, gospodin," the entity said, showing his joy at finding who he thought was his brother again. "Me André, you Hans," he exclaimed. Walker was somewhat nonplussed at the idea of being Hans. "My brother," the entity said, "he killed too. . . . I die . . . big field, battle. Like yesterday, like yesterday . . . I lie here . . . English all over. They are terrible."

"Were you with the Americans?" Dr. Laidlaw asked.

Apparently the word meant nothing to him. "No, no. Big word. Republic. Protection. The stars in the flag, the stars in the flag. Republic. . . . They sing."

"How long have you been hiding in this house?"

"I go away a little, he stays, he talk, he here part of the time."

Uvani returned at this point, taking Andreas out of Eileen's body, explaining that the Polish youngster had been a prisoner. Apparently, he had been in other parts of the country with the French troops. He had been friendly with various people in the

Revolutionary Army, serving as a jackboot for all types of men, a good servant. But he hadn't understood for whom he was working. "He refers to an André," Uvani went on to say, "with whom he is in contact for some time, and he likes this André very much because of the similar name . . . because he is Andrewski. There is this similarity to André. It is therefore he has been used, as far as I can see, as a cover-up for this man. Here then is the confusion. He is caught two or three times by different people because of his appearance; he is a dead-ringer, or double. His friend André disappears, and he's lost and does what he can with this one and that one and eventually he finds himself in the hands of the British troops. He is known to have letters and plans, and these he wants me to tell you were hidden by him due east of where you now find yourselves, in what he says was a temporary building of sorts in which were housed different caissons. In this there is also a rest house for guards. In this type kitchen he will not reveal the plans and is beaten mercilessly. His limbs are broken and he passes out, no longer in the right mind, but with a curious break on one side of the body, and his leg is damaged. It would appear that he is from time to time like one in a coma—he wakes, dreams, and loses himself again, and I gather from the story that he is not always aware of people."

We sat in stunned silence as Uvani explained the story to us. Then we joined in prayer to release the unfortunate one. To the best of my knowledge, the house has been free from further disturbances ever since. The papers, of course, were no longer in their hiding place. French auxiliary troops under Rochambeau and Lafayette had been all over the land, and papers must have gone back and forth between French detachments and their American allies. Some of these papers may have been of lesser importance and could have been entrusted even to so simple a man as Andreas.

The years went by, Danton Walker himself passed away, and the house changed hands, but the pewter jar which Danton had entrusted to my care was still in my hands. Johnny, who had served the late columnist so well for all those years, refused to take it. To him, it meant that the ghost might attach himself to *him* now. Under the circumstances, I kept the jar and placed it in a showcase in my home along with many other antiquities and did not give the matter much thought. But roughly on the twentieth anniversary of the original expedition to the house in Rockland County, I decided to test two good mediums I work with, to see whether any of the past secrets clinging to the pewter might yet be unraveled.

On September 25, 1972, I handed Shawn Robbins a brown paper bag in which the pewter jar had been placed. But Shawn could not make contact, so I took out the object and placed it directly into her hands. "I pick up three initials and a crest," she began. "The first thing I see are these initials, someone's name, like B.A.R.; then I see a man with a beard, and he may have been very important. There is another man, whom I like better, however. They look Nordic to me, because of the strange helmets they wear."

"The person you sense here—is he a civilian or a soldier?"

"I'm thinking of the word 'crown.' There is someone here who wears a crown; the period is the 1700s, perhaps the 1600s. The King wore a crown and a white, high neck, like a ruffled collar, and then armor. That is *one* of the layers I get from this object."

I realized, of course, that the object was already old when the American Revolution took place. Danton Walker had acquired it in the course of his collecting activities, and it had no direct connection with the house itself.

It seemed to me that Shawn was psychometrizing the object quite properly, getting down to the original layer when it was first created. The description of a seventeenth-century English king was indeed quite correct. "The armor is a rough color, but all in one piece and worn over something else, some velvet, I think. On his head, there is a crown, and yet I see him also wearing a hat." I couldn't think of a better description of the way King Charles II dressed, and the pewter pitcher originated during his reign.

"What are some of the other layers you get?" I asked.

"There is a man here who looks as if he either broke his neck or was *hanged*. This man is the strongest influence I feel with this object. He is bearded and slightly baldish in front."

"Stick with him then and try to find out who he was."

Shawn gave the object another thorough investigation, touching it all over with her hands, and then reported, "He is important in the sense that the object is haunted by him. He was murdered by a person who had an object in his hand that looks like a scepter to me, but I don't know what it is. The man in back of him killed him: he got it in the back of his neck. The man who killed him is in a position of power."

"What about the victim—what was his position?"

"The only initials I pick up are something like Pont, or perhaps Boef."

While this did not correspond to Andreas, it seemed interesting to me that she picked up two French names. I recalled that the unlucky Polish jackboot had served the French auxiliaries. "Can you get any country of origin?"

"It is hard to say, but the man who was murdered had something to do with England. Perhaps the man who killed him did."

I then instructed Shawn to put her thumb into the dent in the wall of the pitcher where the ghostly hand of Andreas had made a depression. Again, Shawn came up with the name Boef. Since I wasn't sure whether she was picking up the original owner of the pewter pitcher or perhaps one of its several owners, I asked her to concentrate on the *last* owner and the time during which he had had the object in his house.

"The letter V is an important initial here," she said, "and I sense a boat coming up."

I couldn't help thinking of the sloop *Vulture*, which Major André had wanted to use for his getaway but didn't, and which saved the life of General Arnold. "Do you feel any suffering with this object?" I asked.

"Yes," Shawn replied. "A man was murdered, and a woman was involved: a woman, an older person, and the murderer; this was *premeditated* murder. The victim is a good-looking man, not too old, with a moustache or beard, and it looks as if *they are taking something away from him* which is part of him, something that belonged to him."

"Was it something he had on his person?"

"When he was murdered, he didn't have it on him, and *it is still buried somewhere*," Shawn replied.

Shawn, of course, had no idea that there was a connection between the object she was psychometrizing and the Rockland County Ghost, which I had written about in the 1960s. "What is buried?" I asked, becoming more intrigued by her testimony as the minutes rolled by.

"There is something he owns that is buried somewhere, and I think it goes back to a castle or house. It is not buried inside but *outside*. It is buried near a grave, and whoever buried it was very smart."

"Why was he killed?" I asked.

"I see him, and then another man, besides, who is involved. He was murdered *because he was a friend of this man* and his cause. They are wearing something funny on their heads. One of them is

Major André and the Question of Loyalty   [111]

holding up his two hands, with an object with a face on it, a very peculiar thing."

"Can you tell me where the object he buried is located?"

"I can't describe it unless I can draw it. Give me a pencil. There is the initial 'A' here."

"Who is this 'A'?"

" 'K' would be another initial of importance. This is the hat they are wearing."

Shawn then drew what looked to me like the rough outlines of a fur-braided hat, the kind soldiers in the late eighteenth century would wear in the winter. The initial "A" of course startled me, since it might belong to Andreas. The "K" I thought might refer to Kosciuszko, the leader of the Polish auxiliary forces in America during the Revolutionary War, who wore fur hats. "The hat is part metal, but there is a red feather on it, actually red and green," she said. The colors were quite correct for the period involved.

"This man is in love with an older woman; he is a very good looking fellow. This is how he looks to me." Shawn drew a rough portrait of a man in the wig and short tie of an eighteenth-century gentleman. She then drew the woman also, and mentioned that she wore a flower or some sort of emblem. It reminded her of a flower or a crest and was important. "It is a crude way of saying something, and the letters V.A.R. come in here also. A crest with V.A.R. across it," Shawn said.*

"Tell me, Shawn," I said, steering her in a somewhat different direction, "has there ever been any psychic manifestation associated with this object?"

"Somebody's heavy footsteps are associated with this. Things would move in a house. By themselves."

---

* Richard Varick, of noble Dutch descent, became Aide-de-Camp to General Arnold in August 1780, six weeks prior to the treason. He was not involved in it, however.

"Is there any entity attached to this object?"

"I want to say the name Victor." Was she getting Walker?

As I questioned Shawn further about the object, it became increasingly clear that she was speaking of the period when it was first made. She described, in vivid words, the colors and special designs on the uniforms of the men who were involved with the object. All of it fit the middle or late seventeenth century but obviously had nothing to do with the Revolutionary War. I was not surprised, since I had already assumed that some earlier layer would be quite strong. But then she mentioned a boat and remarked that it was going up a river. "I must be way off on this," Shawn said, somewhat disappointed, "because I see a windmill."

The matter became interesting again. I asked her what became of "A." "There are three or four men in the boat," Shawn said. "They are transporting someone, and I think it is 'A' on his way to his execution."

"What did he do?"

"He didn't do anything—that is the sad part of it. He was just a victim of circumstances. He is an innocent victim."

"Who did his captors think he was?"

"An important person."

"Did this important person commit a crime or did he have something they wanted?"

"He had nothing on him, but the initials K.A.E.A. are of importance here. That is an important name. But they have the wrong man. But they kill him anyway. There is a design on his cloak, which looks to me like the astrological Cancer symbol, like the crab."

"What happens further on?"

"They are leaving the windmill now. But something is going to happen because they are headed that way. Other people are going to die because of this. Many." Without my telling her to, Shawn touched the object again. "I feel the period when Marie Antoinette lived. I have the feeling they are going off in that direction. They are going to France. There is a general here, and I get the initials L.A.M.* He, too, was killed in the war."

"But why is 'A' brought to this general?"

"Well, 'A' looks to me as if he had changed clothes, and now he wears black with a little piece of white here. They are obviously conferring about something. 'A' is conferring with someone else. It doesn't look like someone in the military, and he is hard to describe, but I never saw a uniform like this before. He has on a beret and a medal."

"What about 'A'? Is he a civilian or an officer?"

"Truthfully, he is really an officer. I think this is what the whole thing is all about. I think they captured someone really important. He probably was an officer in disguise, not wearing the right clothing. It is treason, what else? Could he have sold papers, you know, secrets?"

Shawn felt now that she had gotten as much as she could from the object. I found her testimony intriguing, to say the least. There were elements of the André story in it, and traces of Andreas's life as well. Just as confusing, it seemed to me, as the mistaken-identity problems which had caused Andreas's downfall. All this time, Shawn had no idea that Major André was involved in my investigation, no idea of what the experiment was all about. As far as she was concerned, she had been asked to psychometrize an old pewter jar, and nothing else.

On October 3, 1972, I repeated the experiment with Ethel Johnson Meyers. Again, the pitcher was in the brown paper bag. Again, the medium requested to hold it directly in her hands. "I

---

* General John Lamb was sent by General Washington on September 25, 1780, to secure Kings Ferry on the eve of Arnold's treason.

see three women and a man with heavy features," she began immediately. "Something is going on, but the language doesn't sound English. Now there is a man here who is hurt, blood running from his left eye."

"How did he get hurt?"

"There are some violent vibrations here. I hear loud talking, and I feel as if he had been hit with this pitcher. He has on a waistcoat or brown jacket, either plush or velveteen, and a wide collar. Black stockings and purple shoes. Knickers that go down to here, and of the same material as the coat."

"Can you pinpoint the period?"

"I would guess around the time of Napoleon," Ethel said, not altogether sure. That too was interesting since she obviously wasn't judging the jar (which was far older than the Napoleonic period) by its appearance. As far as the Major André incident was concerned, she was about twenty years off. "I am hearing German spoken," Ethel continued. "I think this object has seen death and horror, and I hear violence and screams. There is the feeling of murder, and a woman is involved. I hear a groan, and now there is more blood. I feel there is also a gash on the neck. Once in a while, I hear an English word spoken with a strange accent. I hear the name Mary, and I think this is at least the seventeenth century."

I realized that she was speaking of the early history of the object, and I directed her to tune in on some later vibrations. "Has this object ever been in the presence of a murder?" I asked directly.

"This man's fate is undeserved. He has been crossing over from a far distance into a territory where he is not wanted by many, and he is not worthy of that protection which he has. He has not deserved this; he has no political leanings; he has not offended anyone purposely. His presence is unwanted. God in heaven knows that."

It sounded more and more the way Andreas spoke when Eileen Garrett was his instrument. *Protection!* That was the word he kept repeating, more than any other word, protection from those who would do him injustice and hurt him.

"What nationality is he?"

"It sounds Italian."

"What name does he give you?"

"Rey . . . Rey.* . . . Man betrayed." Ethel was sinking now into a state of semi-trance, and I noticed some peculiar facial changes coming over her; it was almost as if the entity were directing her answers.

"Betrayed by whom?" I asked, bending over to hear every word.

"The ones that make me feel safe."

"Who are they?"

"Bloody Englishmen."

"Who are your friends?"

"I'm getting away from English."

"Is there something this person has that someone else wants?"

"Yes, that is how it is."

"Who is this person to whom all these terrible things are happening?"

"Coming over. A scapegoat."

Again, Ethel managed to touch both the earlier layer and the involvement with the Revolutionary period, but in a confusing and intertwined manner which made it difficult for me to sort out what she was telling me. Still, there were elements that were quite true and which she could not have known, since she, like Shawn, had

---

* And*REas?*

no idea what the object was or why I was asking her to psychometrize it. It was clear to me that no ghostly entity had attached to the object, however, and that whatever the two mediums had felt was in the past. A little lighter in my heart, I replaced the object in my showcase, hoping that it would in time acquire some less violent vibrations from the surrounding objects.

As for Andreas and André, one had a brief moment in the limelight, thanks chiefly to psychical research, while the other is still a major figure in both American and British history. After his execution on October 2, 1780, at Tappan, André was buried at the foot of the gallows. In 1821 his body was exhumed and taken to England and reburied at Westminster Abbey. By 1880 tempers had sufficiently cooled and British-American friendship was firmly enough established to permit the erection of a monument to the event on the spot where the three militia men had come across Major André. Actually, the monument itself was built in 1853, but on the occasion of the centennial of André's capture, a statue and bronze plaque were added and the monument surrounded with a protective metal fence. It stands near a major road and can easily be observed when passing by car. It is a beautiful monument, worthy of the occasion. There is only one thing wrong with it, be it ever so slight: *It stands at the wrong spot.* My good friend, Elliott Schryver, the eminent editor and scholar, pointed out the actual spot at some distance to the east.

In studying Harry Hansen's book on the area, I have the impression that he shares this view. In order to make a test of my own, we stopped by the present monument, and I asked Ingrid to tell me what she felt. I had purposely told her that the spot had no direct connection with anything else we were doing that day, so she could not consciously sense what the meaning of our brief stop was. Walking around the monument two or three times, touching it, and "taking in" the atmosphere psychically, she finally came up to me, shook her head, and said, "I am sorry, Hans, there is absolutely nothing here. Nothing at all."

But why not? If the Revolutionary taverns can be moved a considerable distance to make them more accessible to tourists, why shouldn't a monument be erected where everyone can see it instead of in some thicket where a prospective visitor might break a leg trying to find it? Nobody cares, least of all Major André.

8

Benedict Arnold's Friend

"I was completely fascinated by your recent book," read a letter by Gustav J. Kramer of Claverack, New York. Mr. Kramer, it developed, was one of the leading lights of the Chamber of Commerce in the town of Hudson and wrote a column for the *Hudson Register-Star* on the side. "During the past three years I have specialized in writing so-called ghost stories for my column," he explained. "We have a number of haunted houses in this historic section of the Hudson Valley. President Martin Van Buren's home is nearby and is honestly reputed to be the scene of some highly disturbing influences. Aaron Burr, the killer of Alexander Hamilton, hid out in a secret room of this estate and has reliably been reported to have been seen on numerous occasions wandering through the upper halls."

This was in 1963, and I had not yet investigated the phenomena at Aaron Burr's stables in lower Manhattan at the time. Perhaps what people saw in the house was an imprint of Burr's thought forms.

From this initial letter developed a lively correspondence between us, and for nearly two years I promised to come to the Hudson Valley and do some investigating, provided that Mr. Kramer came up with something more substantial than hearsay.

It wasn't until July 1965 that he came up with what he considered "*the* house." He explained that it had a cold spot in it and that the owner, a Mrs. Dorothea Connacher, a teacher by profession, was a quiet and reserved lady who had actually had a visual experience in the attic of this very old house.

My brother-in-law's untimely and unexpected death postponed our journey once again, so we—meaning Ethel Johnson Meyers, the medium, my wife Catherine, and I—weren't ready to proceed to Columbia County, New York, until early February 1966. GHOST HUNTER VISITS HUDSON, Gus Kramer headlined in his column. He met us at the exit from the Taconic Parkway and took us to lunch before proceeding further.

It was early afternoon when we arrived at Mrs. Connacher's house, which was situated a few minutes away on a dirt road, standing on a fair-sized piece of land and surrounded by tall, old trees. Because of its isolation, one had the feeling of being far out in the country, when in fact the thruway connecting New York with Albany passes a mere ten minutes away. The house is gleaming white, or nearly so, for the ravages of time have taken their toll. Mr. and Mrs. Connacher bought it twenty years prior to our visit, but after divorcing Mr. Connacher, she was unable to keep it up as it should have been, and gradually the interior especially fell into a state of disrepair. The outside still showed its noble past, those typically colonial manor house traits, such as the columned entrance, the Grecian influence in the construction of the roof, and the beautiful colonial shutters.

New York State in the dead of winter is a cold place indeed. As we rounded the curve of the dirt road and saw the manor house looming at the end of a short carriage way, we wondered how the lady of the house was able to heat it. After we were inside, we realized she had difficulties in that respect.

For the moment, however, I halted a few yards away from the house and took some photographs of this visually exciting old house. Ethel Johnson Meyers knew nothing about the house or why we were there. In fact, part of our expedition was for the purpose of finding a country home to live in. Ethel thought we were taking her along to serve as consultant in the purchase of a house, since she herself owns a country home and knows a great deal about houses. Of course, she knew that there were a couple of interesting places en route, but she took that for granted, having worked with me for many years. Even while we were rounding the last bend and the house became visible to us, Ethel started getting her first impressions of the case. I asked her to remain seated in the car and to tell me about it.

"I see two people, possibly a third. The third person is young, a woman with a short, rather upturned nose and large eyes, but she seems to be dimmer than the impression of the men. The men are very strong. One of them has a similar upturned nose and dark skin. He wears a white wig. There is also an older woman. She seems to look at me as if she wants to say, Why are you staring at me that way?" Ethel explained to the spirit in an earnest tone of voice why she had come to the house, that she meant no harm and had come as a friend, and if there were anything she could do for them, they should tell her.

While this one-sided conversation was going on, Catherine and

I sat in the car, waiting for it to end. Gus Kramer had gone ahead to announce our arrival to Mrs. Connacher.

"What sort of clothing is the woman wearing—I mean the older woman?" I asked.

"She's got on some kind of a white dusting cap," Ethel replied, "and her hair is sticking out."

"Can you tell what period they are from?"

"He wears a wig, and she has some sort of kerchief, wide at the shoulders and pointed in back. The blouse of her dress fits tight. The dress goes down to the floor, as far as I can see. The bottom of the dress is ruffled. I should say she is a woman in her sixties, perhaps even older."

"What about the man?"

"I think one of the women could be his daughter, because the noses are alike, sort of pug noses."

"Do you get any names or initials?"

"The letter 'B' is important."

"Do you get any other people?"

"There is a woman with dark hair parted in the middle, and there is a man with a strange hat on his head. Then there is someone with an even stranger hat, octagonal in shape and very high. I've never seen a hat like that before. There is something about a B.A. *A Bachelor of Arts?* Now I pick up the name Ben. I am sorry, but I don't think I can do any more outside."

"In that case," I said, "let us continue inside the house." But I asked Ethel to wait in the car while I interviewed the owner of the house. Afterward, she was to come in and try trance.

Mrs. Dorothea Connacher turned out to be a smallish lady in her later years, and the room we entered first gave the impression of a small, romantic jumble shop. Antiquities, old furniture, a small new stove so necessary on this day, pictures on the walls, books on shelves, and all of it in somewhat less than perfect order made it plain that Mrs. Connacher wasn't quite able to keep up with the times, or rather that the house demanded more work than one person could possibly manage. Mrs. Connacher had been in the house for the past twenty years, and currently lived there with her son, Richmond, age thirty-six. Her husband had left three years after she had moved into the house. I asked her about any psychic experiences she might have had.

"Both my husband and I are freelance artists," she began, "and my husband used to go to New York to work three days a week, and the rest of the time he worked at home. One day shortly after we had moved in, I was alone in the house. That night I had a dream that my husband would leave me. At the time I was so happy I couldn't understand how this could happen."

The dream became reality a short time later. It wasn't the only prophetic dream Mrs. Connacher had. On previous occasions she had had dreams concerning dead relatives and various telepathic experiences.

"What about the house? When did it start here?"

"We were in the house for about five months. We had been told that everything belonging to the former owners had been taken out of the house—there had been an auction, and these things had been sold. There really wasn't anything up in the attic, so we were told. My husband and I had been up a couple of times to explore it. We were fascinated by the old beams, with their wooden pegs dating back to the eighteenth century. There was nothing up there except some old picture frames and a large trunk. It is still up there.

"Well, finally we became curious and opened it, and there were a lot of things in it. It seemed there were little pieces of material all tied up in bundles. But we didn't look too closely; I decided to come up there some day when I had the time to investigate by myself. My husband said he was too busy right then and wanted to go down.

"A few days later, when I was home alone, I decided to go upstairs again and look through the trunk. The attic is rather large, and there are only two very small windows in the far corner. I opened the trunk, put my hands into it, and took out these little pieces of material, but in order to see better I took them to the windows. When I got to the bottom of the trunk, I found a little waistcoat, a hat, and a peculiar bonnet, the kind that was worn before 1800. I thought, what a small person this must have been who could have worn this! At first I thought it might have been for a child; but no, it was cut for an adult, although a very tiny person."

As Mrs. Connacher was standing there, fascinated by the material, she became aware of a pinpoint of light out of the corner of her eye. Her first thought was, I must tell Jim that there is a hole in the roof where this light is coming through. But she kept looking and, being preoccupied with the material in the trunk, paid no attention to the light. Something, however, made her look up, and she noticed that the light had now become substantially larger. Also, it was coming nearer, changing its position all the time. The phenomenon began to fascinate her. She wasn't thinking of ghosts or psychic phenomena at all, merely wondering what this was all about. As the light came nearer and nearer, she suddenly thought, why, that looks like a human figure!

Eventually, it stopped near the trunk, and Mrs. Connacher realized it was a human figure, *the figure of an elderly lady.* She was unusually small and delicate and wore the very bonnet Mrs. Connacher had discovered at the bottom of the trunk! The woman's clothes seemed gray, and Mrs. Connacher noticed the apron the woman was wearing. As she watched the ghostly apparition in fascinated horror, the little lady used her apron in a movement that is generally used in the country to shoo away chickens. However, the motion was directed against *her*, as if the apparition wanted to shoo her away from "her" trunk!

"I was frightened. I saw the bonnet and the apron and this woman shooing me away, and she seemed completely solid," Mrs. Connacher said.

"What did you do?"

"I walked around in back of the trunk to see whether she was still there. She was. I said, all right, all right. But I didn't want to look at her. I could feel my hair stand up and decided to go down. I was worried I might fall down the stairs, but I made it all right."

"Did you ever see her again?"

"No. But there were all sorts of unusual noises. Once my husband and I were about to go off to sleep when it sounded as if someone had taken a baseball bat and hit the wall with it right over our heads. That was in the upstairs bedroom. The spot isn't too far from the attic, next to the staircase."

"Have other people had experiences here?"

"Well, my sister Clair had a dream about the house before she had been here. When she came here for the first time she said she wanted to see *the attic*. I was surprised, for I had not even told her that there *was* an attic. She rushed right upstairs, but when she saw it, she turned around, and her face was white; it was exactly what she had seen in her dream. Then there was this carpenter who had worked for me repairing the attic and doing other chores on the property. After he came down from the attic, he left and hasn't been back since. No matter how often I ask him to come and do some work for me, he never shows up."

"Maybe the little old lady shooed him away too," I said. "What about those cold spots Gus has been telling me about?"

"I only have a fireplace and this small heater here. Sometimes you just can't get the room warm. But there are certain spots in the house that are always cold. Even in the summertime people ask whether we have air conditioning."

"When was the house built?"

"One part has the date 1837 engraved in the stone downstairs. The older part goes back two hundred years."

"Did any of the previous owners say anything about a ghost?"

"No. Before us were the Turners, and before them the Link family owned it for a very long time. But we never talked about such things."

I then questioned Gus Kramer about the house and about his initial discussions with Mrs. Connacher. It is not uncommon for a witness to have a better memory immediately upon telling of an experience than at a later date when the story has been told and told again. Sometimes it becomes embroidered by additional, invented details, but at other times it loses some of its detail because the storyteller no longer cares or has forgotten what he said under the immediate impression of the experience itself.

"Mrs. Connacher was holding an old, musty woman's blouse at the time when the apparition appeared," Gus said. "At the time she felt that there was a connection between her holding this piece of clothing and her sighting."

"Have you yourself ever experienced anything in the Connacher house?"

"Well, the last time I visited here, we were sitting in the dim, cluttered living room, when I noticed the dog follow an imaginary something with his eyes from one bedroom door to the door that leads to the attic, where Mrs. Connacher's experience took place. He then lay down with his head between his paws and his eyes fastened on the attic door. I understand he does this often and very frequently fastens his gaze on 'something' behind Mrs. Connacher's favorite easy chair when she is in it. I assure you, the hairs on the back of my neck stood up like brush bristles while watching that dog."

I decided to get Ethel out of the car, which by now must have become a cold spot of its own. "Ethel," I said, "you are standing in the living room of this house now. There is another story above this one and there is an attic. I want you to tell me if there is any presence in this house and, if so, what area you feel is most affected."

"The top," Ethel replied, without a moment's hesitation.

"Is there a presence there?"

"Yes," Ethel said firmly. We had stepped into the next room, where there was a large, comfortable easy chair. I tried to get Ethel to sit down in it, but she hesitated. "No, I want to go somewhere." I had the distinct impression that she was gradually falling into trance, and I wanted her in a safe chair when the trance took hold. Memories of an entranced Ethel being manipulated by an unruly ghost were too fresh in my mind to permit such chance-taking. I managed to get her back into the chair all right. A moment later, a friendly voice spoke, saying, "Albert, Albert," and I realized that Ethel's control had taken over. But it was a very brief visit. A moment later, a totally different voice came from the medium's entranced lips. At first, I could not understand the words. There was something about a wall. Then a cheery voice broke through. "Who are you, and what the hell are you doing here?"

When you are a psychic investigator, you sometimes answer a question with another question. In this case, I demanded to know who was speaking. "Loyal, loyal," the stranger replied. I assured "him" that we had come as friends and that he—for it sounded like a man—could safely converse with us. "Will you speak to me then?" he asked.

"Can I help you?" I replied.

"Well, I'll help others; they need help."
"Is this your house? Who are you?" But the stranger wouldn't identify himself just yet. "Why were you brought in? Who brought you here?"
"My house, yes. My house, my house."
"What is your name, please?" I asked routinely. Immediately, I felt resistance.
"What is that to you, sir?"
I explained that I wanted to introduce myself properly.
"I'm loyal, loyal," the voice assured me.
"Loyal to whom, may I ask?"
"His Majesty, sir; do you know that George?"
I asked in which capacity the entity was serving His Majesty. "Who are you? You ask for help. Help for what?"
We weren't getting anywhere, it seemed to me. But these things take time, and I have a lot of patience.
"Can you tell me who you are?"
Instead, the stranger became more urgent. "When is he coming, when is he coming? When is he coming to help me?"
"Whom do you expect?" I replied. I tried to assure him that whomever he was expecting would arrive soon, at the same time attempting to find out whom he was talking about. This, of course, put him on his guard.
"I don't say anymore."
Again I asked that he identify himself so I could address him by his proper name and rank.
"You are not loyal, you, you, who are in my house?"
"Well, I was told you needed help."
But the entity refused to give his name. "I fear."
"There is no need to fear. I am a friend. You are making it very difficult for me. I am afraid I cannot stay unless you—" I hinted.
"When will he come? When will he come?"

"Who are you waiting for?"

"Horatio. Horatio Gates. Where is he? Tell me, I am a loyal subject. Where is he? Tell me."

"Well, if you are loyal, you will identify yourself. You have to identify yourself before I can be of any service to you."

Instead, the entity broke into bitter laughter. "My name, ha ha ha. Trap! Trap!"

I assured him it was no trap. "You know me, you do," he said. I assured him that I didn't. "You know me if you come here, ha ha ha."

I decided to try a different tack. "What year are we in?"

This didn't go down well with him either. "Madman, madman. Year, year. You're not of this house. Go."

"Look," I said, "we've come a long distance to speak with you. You've got to be cooperative if we are going to help you." But the stranger insisted, and repeated the question: When will he come? I started to explain that "he" wouldn't come at all, that a lot of time had gone by and that the entity had been "asleep."

Now it was the entity's turn to ask who I was. But before I could tell him again, he cried out, "Ben, where are you?" I wanted to know who Ben was, at the same time assuring him that much time had passed and that the house had changed hands. But it didn't seem to make any impression on him. "Where is he? Are you he? Is that you? Speak to me!" I decided to play along to get some more information. But he realized right away that I was not the one he was expecting. "You are not he, are you he? I can't hang by my throat. I will not hang by my throat. No, no, no."

"Nobody's threatening you. Have you done anything that you fear?"

"My own Lord God knows that I am innocent. If I have a chance. Why, why, why?"

"Who is threatening you? Tell me. I'm on your side."

"But you will get me."

"I've come to help you. This is your house, is it not? What is your name? You have to identify yourself so that I know that I haven't made a mistake," I said, pleading with him. All the time this was going on, Gus Kramer, Mrs. Connacher, and my wife watched in fascinated silence. Ethel looked like an old man now, not at all like her own self. There was a moment of hesitation, a pause. Then the voice spoke again, this time, it seemed to me, in a softer vein.

"Let me be called Anthony."

"Anthony what?"

"Where is he? I wait. I've got to kill him." I explained how it was possible for him to speak to us *in our time*. But it seemed to make no impression on him. "He was here. He was here. I know it."

"Who was here?" I asked, and repeated that he had to identify himself.

"But I may go?" There was a sense of urgency in his voice.

"Would you like to leave this house?"

"My house, why my house? To hang here. My daughter, she may go with you."

"What is your daughter's name?"

"Where you lead, I go, she says. But she too will hang here if I do not go. She too. God take me, you will take me."

I assured him that he could leave the house safely and need not return again. "You will be safe. You'll see your daughter again. But you must understand, there is no more war. No more killing."

"She died right here, my sweet daughter, she died right here."

"What happened to you after that?"

"I sit here; you see me. I sit here. I will go."

"How old are you?"

"I'm not so old that I can't go from here, where the fields are fertile, and oh! no blood."

"Where would you like to go from here?"

"Far away. Sweet Jennie died. Take me from here. He does not come."

"I promise to take you. Just be calm."

"Oh, Horatio, Horatio, you have promised. Why did he come instead of you, Horatio?"

"Did you serve under Horatio Gates?"

"Arnold, are you he? No."

"If you're looking for Arnold, he's dead."

"You lie."

Again, I explained, tactfully, about the passage of time. But he would hear none of it.

"You lie to me. He will come. You lie."

"No," I replied. "It is true. Arnold is dead."

"Why? Why, why, why? He is gone, is he?"

"Is your name Anthony?"

Eagerly he replied: "Oh, yes, it is. They don't want me to go from here, but I must go, they'll hang me. Don't let them hang me." I assured him that I wouldn't. "My daughter, my sweet child. Oh why, because we swear allegiance to . . . Now I hang here. They will come to get me; they will come. Where is he? He has forsaken me."

"A lot of time has gone by. You have passed on."

"No. Madness. John, John, help me. Come quick."

I informed the entity that he was speaking through a female instrument, and to touch his instrument's hair. That way, he would be convinced that it wasn't his own body he was in at present.

"John, John, where are you? I'm dreaming."

I assured him that he wasn't dreaming, and that I was speaking the truth.

"I am mad, I am mad."

I assured him that he was sane.

"They hold me. Oh, Jesus Christ!"

I began the usual rescue-circle procedure, explaining that by wanting to be with his daughter, who had gone on before him, he could leave this house where his tragedy had kept him. "Go from this house. You are free to join your daughter. Go in peace; we'll pray for you. There is nothing to fear." A moment later, the entity was gone and Albert had returned to Ethel Meyers's body.

Usually, I question Albert, the control personality, concerning any entity that has been permitted to speak through Ethel Meyers's instrumentality. Sometimes additional information or the previous information in more detailed and clarified form emerges from these discussions. But Albert explained that he could not give me the man's name. "He gives false names. As far as we can judge here, he believes he was hanged. He was a Loyalist, refusing to take refuge with Americans. He didn't pose as a Revolutionary until the very end, when he thought he could be saved." Albert explained that this had taken place in this house during the Revolutionary War.

"Why does he think he was hanged? Was he?"

"I don't see this happening in this house. I believe he was taken from here, yes."

"What about other entities in this house?"

"There have been those locked in secret here, who have had reason to be here. They are all still around. There is a woman who died and who used to occupy this part of the house and up to the next floor. Above, I think I hear those others who have been wounded and secreted here."

I asked Albert if he could tell us anything further about the woman who had been seen in the house. "I remember I showed this to my instrument before. She was wearing a white, French-like kerchief hat with lace and little black ribbons. There are two women, but one is the mother to this individual here. I am talking about the older woman."

"Why is she earthbound?"

"Because she passed here and remained simply because she wanted to watch her husband's struggles to save himself from being dishonored and discredited. Her husband is the one who was speaking to you."

"Can you get anything about the family?"

"They have been in this country for some time, and they are Loyalists."

"Why is the woman up there in the attic and not down here in the rest of the house?"

"She comes down, but she stays above, for she passed there."

"Do you get her name?"

"Elsa, or Elva."

"Is she willing to speak to us?"

"I can try, but she is a belligerent person. You see, she keeps reliving her last days on earth, and then the hauntings in her own house, while her husband and daughter were still living here. Sometimes they clash one with the other."

"What about the other woman? Can you find out anything about her?"

"I can describe her, but I can't make her speak. She has dark hair parted in the middle and an oval face, and she wears a high-necked dress of a dark color. Black with long sleeves, I think. However, I feel she is from a later period."

"Why is she earthbound in the house?"

"She had been extremely psychic when she lived here, and she has been bothered by these other ghosts that were here before her.

Her name was Drew. Perhaps Andrew, although I rather think Drew was the family name. She died in this house. There was a man who went before her. A curse had been put on her by a woman who was here before her. It was a ghostly kind of quarrel between the two women. One was angry that she should be here, and the other was angry because she owned the house and found it invaded by those unwanted 'guests,' as she called them."

I asked Albert to make sure that the house was now "clean" and to bring Ethel back to her own self. "I will not need to take the woman by the hand," he explained. "She will go away with her husband, now that he has decided to leave for fear they will hang him." With that, I thanked Albert for his help, and Ethel returned to herself a few moments later, remembering nothing of what had transpired, as is usual with her when she is in deep trance.

We had not yet been to the upper part of the house. Even though Ethel would normally be quite tired after a trance session, I decided to have a look at the second story and the attic. Ethel saw a number of people in the upper part of the house, both presences and psychometric impressions from the past. I felt reasonably sure that the disturbed gentleman who had called himself Anthony was gone from the house, as was his daughter. There remained the question of the other woman, the older individual who had frightened Mrs. Connacher. "I see what looks like a small boy," Ethel suddenly exclaimed as we were standing in the attic. "I rather think it is a woman, a short woman."

"Describe her, please."

"She seems to wear a funny sort of *white cap*. Her outfit is pinkish gray, with a white handkerchief over her shoulders going down into her belt. She looks like a girl and is very small, but she is an older woman, nevertheless."

En route to another house at Hudson, New York, I asked Gus

Kramer to comment. "Benedict Arnold was brought to this area after the battle of Saratoga to recuperate for one or two nights," Kramer explained, and I reminded myself that General Arnold, long before he turned traitor to the American cause, had been a very successful field commander and administrative officer on the side of the Revolution. "He spent the night in the Kinderhook area," Gus continued. "The location of the house itself is not definitely known, but it is known that he spent the night here. Horatio Gates, who was the American leader in the battle of Saratoga, also spent several nights in the immediate area. It is not inconceivable that this place, which was a mansion in those days, might have entertained these men at the time."

"What about the hanging?"

"Seven Tories were hanged in this area during the Revolutionary War. Some of the greatest fighting took place here, and it is quite conceivable that something took place at this old mansion. Again, it completely bears out what Mrs. Meyers spoke of while in trance."

I asked Gus to pinpoint the period for me. "This would have been in 1777, toward October and November."

"What about that cold spot in the house?"

"Outside of the owner," Gus replied, "there was an artist named Stanley Bate, who visited the house and complained about an unusually cold spot. There was one particular room that was known as the Sick Room; we have found out from a later investigation that it is one of the bedrooms upstairs. It was used for mortally sick people, when they became so ill that they had to be brought to this bedroom, and eventually several of them died in it. You couldn't notice it today, because the whole house was so cold, but we have noticed a difference of at least twenty-five to thirty degrees in the temperature between that room and the surrounding part of the house. This cannot be attributed to drafts or open windows."

"Did your artist friend who visited the house experience anything else besides the cold spot?"

"Yes, he had a very vivid impression of someone charging at him several times. There was a distinct tugging on his shirt sleeve. This was about two years ago, and though he knew that the house was haunted, he had not heard about the apparition Mrs. Connacher had seen."

It appeared to me that the entity, Anthony, or whatever his name might have been, had pretty good connections on both sides of the Revolutionary War. He was in trouble, that much was clear. In his difficulty, he turned to Benedict Arnold, and he turned to General Horatio Gates, both American leaders. He also cried out to John to save him, and I can't help wondering, common though the name is, whether he might not also have known Major John André.

9

The Haverstraw Ferry Case

Haverstraw is a sleepy little town about an hour's ride from New York City, perched high on the west side of the Hudson River. As its name implies, it was originally settled by the Dutch. On the other side of the river, not far away, was Colonel Beverley Robinson's house, where Benedict Arnold made his headquarters. The house burned down some years ago, and today there are only a few charred remnants to be seen on the grounds. At Haverstraw also was the house of Joshua Smith, the man who helped Major John André escape, having been entrusted with the British spy's care by his friend, Benedict Arnold. At Haverstraw, too, was one of the major ferries to cross the Hudson River, for during the Revolutionary period there were as yet no bridges to go from one side to the other.

I had never given Haverstraw any particular thought, although

The Haverstraw Ferry Case

I had passed through it many times on my way upstate. In August 1966 I received a letter from a gentleman named Jonathan Davis, who had read some of my books and wanted to let me in on an interesting case he thought worthy of investigation. The house in question stands directly on the river, overlooking the Hudson and, as he put it, practically in the shadow of High Tor. Including the basement, there are four floors in all. But rather than give me the information secondhand, he suggested to the owner, a friend, that she communicate with me directly. The owner turned out to be Laurette Brown, an editor of a national women's magazine in New York City.

"I believe my house is haunted by one or possibly two ghosts: a beautiful thirty-year-old girl and her two-year-old daughter," she explained. Miss Brown had shared the house with another career girl, Kaye S., since October 1965. Kaye, a lovely blonde girl who came from a prominent family, was extremely intelligent and very creative. She adored the house overlooking the river, which the two women had bought on her instigation. Strangely, though, Kaye frequently said she would never leave it again *alive*. A short time later, allegedly because of an unhappy love affair, she drove her car to Newburgh, rigged up the exhaust pipe, and committed suicide along with the child she had had by her second husband.

"After she died, and I lived here alone, I was terribly conscious of a spirit trying to communicate with me," Miss Brown explained. "There was a presence, there were unnatural bangings of doors and mysterious noises, but I denied them. At the time, I wanted no part of the so-called supernatural." Since then, Miss Brown has had second thoughts about the matter, especially as the phenomena continued. She began to wonder whether the restless spirit wanted something from her, whether there was something she could do for the spirit. One day, her friend Jonathan Davis was visiting and mentioned that he very much wanted the red rug on which he was standing at the time and which had belonged to Kaye. Before Miss Brown could answer him, Davis had the chilling sensation of a presence and the impression that a spirit was saying to him, "No, you may not take *my rug*."

"Since that time, I have also heard footsteps, and the crying of a child. Lately, I wake up, out of a deep sleep, around midnight or 2:00 A.M., under the impression that someone is trying to reach me. This has never happened to me before."

Miss Brown then invited me to come out and investigate the matter. I spoke to Jonathan Davis and asked him to come along on the day when my medium and I would pay the house a visit. Davis contributed additional information. According to him, on the night of August 6, 1966, when Miss Brown had awakened from deep sleep with particularly disturbed thoughts, she had gone out on the balcony overlooking the Hudson River. At the same time, she mixed herself a stiff drink to calm her nerves. As she stood on the balcony with her drink in hand, she suddenly felt another presence with her, and she knew at that instant, had she looked to the right, she would have seen a person. She quickly gulped down her drink and went back to sleep. She remembered, as Mr. Davis pointed out, that her former housemate had strongly disapproved of her drinking.

"It may interest you to know," Miss Brown said, "that the hills around High Tor Mountain, which are so near to our house, are reputed to be inhabited by a race of dwarves that come down from the mountains at night and work such mischief as moving road signs, et cetera. That here is some feeling of specialness, even enchantment, about this entire area, Kaye always felt, and I believe that if spirits can roam the earth, hers is here at the house she so loved."

The story sounded interesting enough, even though I did not take Miss Brown's testimony at face value. As is always the case when a witness has preconceived notions about the origin of a psychic disturbance, I assume nothing until I have investigated the case myself. Miss Brown had said nothing about the background of the house. From my knowledge of the area, I knew that there were many old houses still standing on the river front.

Ethel Johnson Meyers was my medium, and Catherine, as on so many other occasions, drove the car. My wife, who had by then become extremely interested in the subject, helped me with the tape recording equipment and the photography. Riverside Avenue runs along the river but is a little hard to locate if you don't know your way around Haverstraw. The medium-size house turned out to be quite charming, perched directly on the water's edge. Access to it was now from the street side, although I felt pretty sure that the main entrance had been either from around the corner or from the water itself. From the looks of the house, it was immediately clear to me that we were dealing with a pre-Revolutionary building.

Miss Brown let us into a long verandah running alongside the house, overlooking the water. Adjacent to it was the living room, artistically furnished and filled with antiquities, rugs, and pillows. Mr. Davis could not make it after all, owing to some unexpected business in the city.

Ethel Meyers sat down in a comfortable chair in the corner of the living room, taking in the appointments with the eye of a woman who has furnished her own home not so long before. She knew nothing about the case or the nature of our business here.

"I see three men and a woman," she began. "The woman has a big nose and is on the older side; one of the men has a high forehead; and then there is a man with a smallish kind of nose, a round face, and long hair. This goes back some time, though."

"Do you feel an actual presence in this house?"

"I feel as if someone is looking at me from the back," Ethel replied. "It might be a woman. I have a sense of disturbance. I feel as if I wanted to run away—I'm now speaking as if I were *her*, you understand—I'm looking for the moment to run, to get away."

Ethel took a deep breath and looked toward the verandah, and beyond it to the other side of the Hudson River. "Somebody stays here *who keeps looking out a window* to see if anyone is coming. I can't seem to find the window. There is a feeling of panic. It feels as if I were afraid of somebody's coming. A woman and two men are involved. I feel I want to protect someone."

"Let the individual take over, then, Ethel," I suggested, hoping that trance would give us further clues.

But Ethel wasn't quite ready for it. "I've got to find that window," she said. "She is full of determination to find that window."

"Why is the window so important to her?"

"She wants to know if someone is coming. She's got to look out the window."

I instructed Ethel to tell the spirit that we would look for the window, and to be calm. But to the contrary, Ethel seemed more and more agitated. "Got to go to the window . . . the window . . . the window. The window isn't here anymore, but I've got to find it. Who took away the. . . . No, it is not here. It is not this way. It is that way." By now Ethel was gradually sinking into trance, although by no means a complete one. At certain moments she was still speaking as herself, giving us her clairvoyant impressions, while at other moments some alien entity was already speaking through her directly.

"Very sick here, very sick," she said, her words followed by deep moaning. For several minutes I spoke to the entity directly, explaining that whatever he was now experiencing was only the passing symptoms remembered and had no validity in the present.

The Haverstraw Ferry Case

The moaning, however, continued for some time. I assured the entity that he could speak to me directly, and that there was nothing to be afraid of, for we had come as friends.

Gradually, the moaning became quieter, and individual words could be understood. "What for? What for? The other house . . ." This was immediately followed by a series of moans. I asked who the person was and why he was here, as is my custom. "Why are you bringing him here?" the entranced medium said. "That man, that man, why are you bringing him here? Why? Why?" This was followed by heavy tears.

As soon as I could calm the medium again, the conversation continued. "What troubles you? What is your problem? I would like to help you," I said. "Talk, talk, talk . . . too many . . . too many."

"Be calm, please."

"No! Take him away! I can't tell. They have left. Don't touch me! Take it away! Why hurt me so?"

"It's all right now; much has happened since," I began.

Heavy tears was the response. "They went away. Don't bother me! They have gone. Don't touch! Take him away! Take them off my neck!"

"It's all right," I said again, in as soothing a tone of voice as I could muster. "You are free. You need not worry or fear anything."

Ethel's voice degenerated into a mumble now. "Can't talk . . . so tired . . . go away."

"You may talk freely about yourself."

"I'll tell you when they've gone. I didn't help. . . . I didn't help. . . . I didn't know."

"Who are the people you are talking about?"

"I don't know. They took it over."

"Tell me what happened."

"They went away over the water. Please take this off so I can talk better."

Evidently, the entity thought that he was still gagged or otherwise prevented from speaking clearly. In order to accommodate him, I told him I was taking off whatever was bothering him, and he could speak freely and clearly now. Immediately, there was a moaning sound, more of relief than of pain. But the entity would not believe that I had taken "it" off and called me a liar instead. I tried to explain that he was feeling a memory from the past, but he did not understand that. Eventually he relented.

"What is your name?" I asked.

"You know, you know." Evidently he had mistaken me for someone else. I assured him that I did not know his name.

"You are a bloody rich man, that is what you are," he said, not too nicely. Again, he remembered whatever was preventing him from speaking, and, clutching his throat, cried, "I can't speak . . . the throat . . ." Then, suddenly, he realized there was no more pain and calmed down considerably. "I didn't have that trouble after all," he commented.

"Exactly. That is why we've come to help you."

"Enough trouble. . . . I saw them come up, but they went away."

All along I had assumed that we were talking to a male. Since the entity was using Ethel's voice, there were of course some female tinges to it, but somehow it sounded more like a masculine voice than that of a woman. But it occurred to me that I had no proof one way or another.

"What is your name? Are you a gentleman or . . ."

"Defenseless woman. Defenseless. I didn't take anyone. But you won't believe me."

I assured her that I would.

The Haverstraw Ferry Case

"You won't believe me. . . . It was dark. It was dark here. . . . I told him, take care of me."

"Is this your house?"

"Yes."

"What is your name?"

"My name is Jenny."

"Why are you here?"

"Where is my window? Where is it?"

I ignored the urgency of that remark and continued with my questioning. "What is your family name?"

"Smith . . . Smith."

"Where and when were you born?"

There was no reply.

"What day is this today?" I continued.

"July."

"What year are we in?"

" '80."

"What went on in this house? Tell me about it."

"They brought him here. They came here." Evidently the woman wasn't too happy about what she was about to tell me.

"Whose house is this?"

"Joshua. Joshua Smith."

"How is he related to you?"

"Husband. They brought him. . . . I told them, tell them! No . . . no one was coming. That is all I told them. I don't know why they hurt me."

"You mean, they thought you knew something?"

"Yah . . . my friends. All that noise. Why don't they stop? Oh, God, I feel pain. They got away. I told you they got away."

"Who are the people you fear?"

"Guns—I must look in the window. They are coming. All is clear . . . time to go . . . they get away . . . they got away.

... See, look, they got away. It is dark. They are near the water. I get the money for it."

"What is the money for?"

"For helping."

At the time, I hadn't fully realized the identity of the speaker. I therefore continued the interrogation in the hope of ferreting out still more evidential material from her. "Who is in charge of this country?"

"George . . . George . . . nobody . . . *everybody is fighting.*"

"Where were you born?"

"Here."

"Where was your husband born?"

Instead of answering the question, she seemed to say, faintly but unmistakably, "André."

"Who is André?"

"He got away. *God Bless His Majesty.* He got away."

"You must go in peace from this house," I began, feeling that the time had come to free the spirit from its compulsion. "Go in peace and never return here, because much time has gone on since, and all is peaceful now. You mustn't come back. You mustn't come back."

"They will come back."

"Nobody will come. It all happened a long time ago. Go away from here."

"Johnny . . . Johnny . . ."

"You are free, you are free. You can go from this house."

"Suckers . . . bloody suckers. . . . They are coming, they are coming now. I can see them. I can see them! God Bless the Majesty. They got away, they got away!"

It was clear that Jenny was reliving the most dramatic moment of her life. Ethel, fully entranced now, sat up in the chair, eyes

The Haverstraw Ferry Case [145]

glazed, peering into the distance, *as if she were following the movements of people we could not see!*

"There is the horse," the spirit continued. "Quick, get the horse! I am a loyal citizen. Good to the Crown. They got away. Where is my window?" Suddenly, the entity realized that everything wasn't as it should be. An expression of utter confusion crept over Ethel's face. "Where am I, where am I?"

"You are in a house that now belongs to someone else," I explained.

"Where is that window? I don't know where I am."

I continued to direct her away from the house, suggesting that she leave in peace and go with our blessings. But the entity was not quite ready for that yet. She wouldn't go out the window, either. "The soldiers are there."

"Only in your memory," I assured her, but she continued to be very agitated.

"Gone . . . a rope. . . . My name is Jenny. . . . Save me, save me!"

At this point, I asked Albert to help free the entity, who was obviously tremendously embroiled in her emotional memories. My appeal worked. A moment later, Albert's crisp, matter-of-fact voice broke through. "We have taken the entity who was lost in space and time," he commented.

If ever there was proof that a good trance medium does not draw upon the unconscious minds of the sitters—that is to say, those in the room with her—then this was it. Despite the fact that several names had come through Ethel's entranced lips, I must confess they did not ring a bell with me. This is the more amazing as I am an historian and should have recognized the name Joshua Smith. But the fact is, in the excitement of the investigation, I did not, and I continued to press for better identification and background. In fact, I did not even connect John with André and continued to ask who John was. Had we come to the house with some knowledge that a Revolutionary escape had taken place here, one might conceivably attribute the medium's tremendous performance to unconscious or even conscious knowledge of what had occurred in the place. As it was, however, we had come because of a suspected ghost created only a few years ago—a ghost that had not the slightest connection with pre-Revolutionary America. No one, including the owner of the house, had said anything about any historical connotations of the house. Yet, instead of coming up with the suspected restless girl who had committed suicide, Mrs. Meyers went back into the eighteenth century and gave us authentic information—information I am sure she did not possess at the time, since she is neither a scholar specializing in pre-Revolutionary Americana nor familiar with the locality or local history.

When Albert took over the body of the instrument, I was still in the dark about the connections between this woman and Smith and André. "Albert," I therefore asked with some curiosity, "who is this entity?"

"There are three people here," Albert began. "One is gone on horseback, and one went across. They came here to escape because they were surrounded. One of them was Major André."

"The historical Major André?" I asked incredulously.

"Yes," Albert replied. "They took asylum here until the coast was clear, but as you may well know, André did not get very far, and Arnold escaped across the water."

"What about the woman? Is her real name Smith?"

"Yes, but she is not related to Joshua Smith. She is a woman in charge of properties, living here."

"Why does she give the name Jenny Smith?"

"She was thinking more of her employer than of herself. She worked for Joshua Smith, and her name was Jennifer."

"I see," I said, trying to sort things out. "Have you been able to help her?"

"Yes, she is out of a vacuum now, thanks to you. We will of course have to watch her until she makes up her mind that it is no longer 1780."

"Are there any others here in the house?" I asked.

"There are others. The Tories were always protected around this neck of the woods, and when there was an escape, it was usually through here."

"Are all the disturbances in this house dating back to the colonial period?"

"No, there are later disturbances here right on top of old disturbances."

"What is the most recent disturbance in this house?"

"A woman and a child."

Immediately this rang a bell. It would have been strange if the medium had not also felt the most recent emotional event in this house, that involving a woman and a child. According to Jonathan Davis, Miss Brown had heard the sound of a child in a room that was once used as a nursery. Even her young daughter, then age five, had heard the sounds and been frightened by them. But what about the woman?

"The woman became very disturbed because of the entity you have just released," Albert responded. "In fact, she had been taken over. This was not too long ago."

"What happened to her?"

"She became possessed by the first woman, Jennifer, and as a result felt very miserable."

"Am I correct in assuming that Jennifer, the colonial woman, was hanged?"

"That is right."

"And am I further correct in assuming that the more recent woman took on the symptoms of the unfortunate Jennifer?"

"That is right, too."

"I gather Jennifer died in this house. How?"

"Strangulation."

"What about the more recent case? How did she die?"

"Her inner self was tortured. She lost her breath. She was badly treated by men who did not understand her aberration, the result of her possession by the first spirit in the house. Thus, she committed suicide. It was poison or strangulation or both, I am not sure."

"Do you still sense her in the house now?"

"Yes. She is always following people around. She is here all right, but we did not let her use the instrument, because she could stay on, you know. However, we have her here, under control. She is absolutely demented now. At the time she committed suicide, she was possessed by this woman, but we cannot let her speak because she would possess the instrument. Wait a moment. All right, thank you, they have taken her." Evidently, Albert had been given the latest word by his helpers on the Other Side. It appeared that Kaye was in safe hands, after all.

"Is there any connection between this woman and the present occupants of the house?" I asked.

"Yes, but there will be no harm. She was not in the right mind when she died, and she is not yet at rest. I'm sure she would want to make it clear that she was possessed and did not act as herself. Her suicide was not of her own choosing. I am repeating words I am being told: *it was not of her own volition.* She suffered terribly from the possession, because the colonial woman had been beaten and strangled by soldiers."

"Before you withdraw, Albert, can we be reasonably sure that the house will be quiet from now on?"

"Yes. We will do our best."

With that, Albert withdrew, and Ethel returned to her own self, seemingly a bit puzzled at first as to where she was, rubbing her eyes, yawning a couple of times, then settling back into the comfortable chair and waiting for me to ask further questions, if any. But for the moment I had questions only for the owner of the house. "How old is this house, and what was on the spot before it was built?"

"It is at least a hundred years old, and I remember someone telling me that something happened down here on this spot, something historical, like an escape. There were soldiers here during the Revolutionary War, but I really don't know exactly what happened."

It is important to point out that even Miss Brown, who had lived in the area for some time, was not aware of the full background of her house. The house, in fact, was far more than a hundred years old. It stood already in September 1780, when Major John André had visited it. At that time, there was a ferry below the house that connected with the opposite shore, and the house itself belonged to Joshua Smith, a good friend of General Benedict Arnold. It was to Joshua Smith that Arnold had entrusted the escape of Major André. Everything Ethel had said was absolutely true. Three people had tried to escape: André, a servant, and, of course, General Arnold, who succeeded. Smith was a Loyalist and considered his help a matter of duty. To the American Army he was a traitor. Even though André was later captured, the Revolutionary forces bore down heavily on Smith and his property. Beating people to death in order to elicit information was a favorite form of treatment used in the eighteenth century by both the British and the American armies. Undoubtedly, Jennifer had been the victim of Revolutionary soldiers, and Kaye, perhaps psychic herself, the victim of Jennifer.

Ethel Meyers had once again shown what a superb medium she is. But there were still some points to be cleared up.

"How long have you had the house now, Miss Brown?" I asked.

"A year and a half. Kaye's suicide took place after we had been here for two months. We had bought the house together. She had been extremely upset because her husband was going to cut off his support. Also, he had announced a visit, and she didn't want to see him. So she took off on a Sunday with her child, and in Newburgh she committed suicide along with the child. They didn't find her until Thursday."

"After her death, what unusual things did you experience in the house?"

"I always felt that someone was trying to communicate with me, and I was fleeing from it in terror. I still feel her presence here, but now I *want* it to be here. She always said that she wanted to stay here, that she loved this river bank. We both agreed that she would always stay here. When I heard all sorts of strange noises after her death, such as doors closing by themselves and footsteps where no one could be seen walking, I went into an alcoholic oblivion and on a sleeping-pill binge, because I was so afraid. At the time, I just didn't want to communicate."

"Prior to these events, did you have any psychic experiences?"

"I had many intuitive things happen to me, such as knowing things before they happened. I would know when someone was dead before I got the message; for instance, prior to your coming, I had heard noises almost every night and felt the presence of people. My little girl says there is a little Susan upstairs, and sometimes I too hear her cry. I hear her call and the way she walks up and down the stairs."

"Did you ever think that some of this might come from an earlier period?"

"No, I never thought of that."

"Was Kaye the kind of person who might commit suicide?"

"Certainly not. It would be completely out of character for her. She used to say, there was always a way, no matter what the problem, no matter what the trouble. She was very optimistic, very reliable, very resourceful. And she considered challenges and problems things one had to surmount. After her death, I looked through the mail, through all her belongings. My first impression was that she had been murdered, because it was so completely out of character for her. I even talked to the police about it. Their investigation was in my opinion not thorough enough. They never looked into the matter of where she had spent the four days and four nights between Sunday and Thursday, before she was found. But I was so broken up about it myself, I wasn't capable of conducting an investigation of my own. For a while I even suspected her husband of having killed her."

"But now we know, don't we," I said.

The ferry at Haverstraw hasn't run in a long, long time. The house on Riverside Avenue still stands, quieter than it used to be, and it is keeping its secrets locked up tight now. The British and the Americans have been fast friends for a long time now, and the passions of 1780 belong to history.

10

A Visit to Oley Forge

Richard Shaner, a schoolteacher who lives in the Pennsylvania Dutch country, brought an interesting case to my attention. He wrote me a letter that read, "My wife and I live in a colonial mansion built in 1750 by an ironmaster who was also a colonel in the American Revolution. We have reason to believe that a secret passageway was built in the vicinity of the mansion and that the home is possessed by spirits."

Shaner bought Oley Forge in order to save it from vandals. It was built on the Manatawny Creek in 1744 by Colonel John Lesher, and it is not far from Pleasantville, deep in the heart of the Pennsylvania Dutch country and equidistant from New York City and Philadelphia. Traveling in the direction of Lancaster, one takes a side road which in turn leads to an even smaller road, and

A Visit to Oley Forge

through a number of tricky bends and cutoffs one eventually arrives in a shaded valley at the bottom of which stands the house.

There is an infrequent connection to this area via Kutztown, but I did not want to rely on local transportation. Fortunately, an attractive young lady who has assisted me in some of my investigations, Sherry Wright, offered to drive me to Oley, and she drove so well we arrived fifteen minutes ahead of time.

The Shaners had restored the old house with much love and, I am sure, much expense, so that it now looks exactly the way it did when Colonel Lesher lived in it. It is a two-story stone house on a flat piece of land, with windows reaching down to the floor level the way they did in the eighteenth century. When one approaches the house, one passes an old wagon of the kind that even now can be seen in the Amish country, among people who have no use for the modern automobile. To the right of the house is an overgrown area which was once part of the gardens but has since pretty much returned to nature. There are some remnants of slave quarters and other out-buildings that the Shaners have not yet had time to restore. On the other side of the little creek and connected with the house by a narrow footbridge are the remnants of the iron works. The whole area has been subjected to a number of archeological expeditions by Shaner and his pupils. They have managed to discover a large number of artifacts, especially broken pottery, iron tools, and glass. Shaner has reported on his findings in the *Historical Review of Berks County*, and they are now on exhibit at the local museum.

The house is furnished in eighteenth-century style. Much of the furniture is authentic; the rest is new but follows the eighteenth-century model to the hilt. There are four-posters in the bedrooms, Pennsylvania Dutch chests, handmade and hand painted, and a long wooden table in the dining room which reminds one of paintings showing life in colonial days. In one of the bedrooms there is a spinning wheel. The only modern touches are the electric light and the telephone.

John Lesher, the builder of the house, was a wagon master in the French and Indian War and was later commissioned a forager for Washington's troops. As Colonel Lesher, he became a delegate to Pennsylvania's Constitutional Convention in 1776 and served three terms in the state legislature. In his ironworking business, he was partnered with his father-in-law, John Yoder, and a Philadelphia gentleman named John Ross. Ross, an influential person in Philadelphia's colonial society, was an attorney by profession and brother to George Ross, one of the signers of the Declaration of Independence; the Rosses also were uncles of Betsy Ross, who made the first United States flag.

Richard Shaner teaches psychology at the local high school; his interest in parapsychology goes back some years and is coupled with a strong interest in sociology and archeology. After our arrival at Oley Forge, I asked Shaner to give Sherry and me a quick tour of the house. In particular, I wanted to be shown the areas where psychic phenomena had occurred before I learned about any of the specific details of the case. I wanted to find out whether Sherry or I would sense anything special in those locations.

Shaner explained that the house was a ruin when they had bought it four years before. They had had to do the entire house over: plaster it, paint it, and bring it back to its original condition. Prior to their acquisition, the house had been in various hands. Eventually, the owners of a nearby farm acquired the property, but there was a long-drawn-out dispute over the inheritance, and so the estate was never settled. Because of that, no one had been able to buy the house for many years. Originally, there had been sixty acres to the property, but the Shaners had bought only two and had taken an option on the barn, which is also quite dilapidated. They were thinking of acquiring more land where the iron forge originally stood; there are no traces of the forge left, as a heavy flood around the turn of this century swept away all of its ruins.

The rear wall of the second story has a peculiar window; on close inspection, it turned out to be a former door. Shaner explained that iron used to be brought up through that door in the old days and deposited in the hallway. Later, when iron ore was no longer being mined, the room was turned into a second bedroom, and the door became a window. I noticed a large four-poster bed in the room, and in the center of the bedspread, which Shaner's mother had made, was a Pennsylvania hex sign. A peculiar hole in the wall, fairly high up, attracted my attention.

"That is a *soul window*," Shaner explained. "When you die, your soul goes through the hole and up to heaven. Colonel Lesher employed some Irish 'indentured' workers, and the Irish believe in such things. Had the Colonel died at the house, he would have been taken to the kitchen and the hole would then have been opened up so that his soul could have gone to heaven."

We were now standing in what looked like a kitchen to me. "This is what they used to call the preparation kitchen," Shaner confirmed. "If the master was home alone, he would eat here; when the whole family was together, they dined in the dining room next door. You see this strange stove? This was called a German stove, and it consists of an iron box on the other side of this wall into which hot coals from the fireplace in this room could be thrown, so that the dining room would be heated as well. Every room in the house except the dining room has a fireplace."

"Well, now," I said, after we had returned to the dining room and seated ourselves in the comfortable chairs standing in the four corners of it, "what exactly took place here that convinced you that you had psychic phenomena in the house?"

"Teenagers used to call the house 'haunted' for years before we ever got here," Shaner explained, "and for miles around, the place had the reputation of being haunted. It had always attracted me somehow. After we bought it, I often wondered how we were able to restore everything so quickly and so well, pretty much the way it had been in the past. Colonel Lesher had mainly Irishmen from the old country working here. When I became infatuated with everything Irish, I began to wonder about it, until I spoke to my father and found that my own grandfather had been part Irish. That was in 1969, and I was already very much interested in extrasensory perception. I wondered whether it might be possible to hold a séance in the house and discover something about its past. We decided to hold it on Halloween, and I asked my students to try to find me a good medium."

All the students came up with were local gypsies, honest enough to admit they weren't mediums at all. When the date for the séance drew nearer and nearer, and Shaner still had not located an appropriate medium, he sought the help of a newspaper reporter named Ann Capalanko. The reporter had some connections in the psychic world and promised to secure a medium.

It was a few days before Halloween, and Shaner was in bed. Shortly before eleven, the telephone rang downstairs. It was the reporter, informing him that she had found a medium, a Mrs. Terrell. Pleased with this news, Shaner hung up the phone and went back up to bed. As he pulled the covers over himself, a strong breeze shook them from his hands. There was no logical explanation for this, so Shaner thought that "someone" in the house was apparently pleased that they were going to have a séance. At the time, the house had not been fully restored, and Shaner lived in it by himself.

"What happened on Halloween?" I asked.

"My students were most anxious about the whole thing; we had decorated the house with candlelight. The medium, Helen Terrell, came all the way from Bethlehem, Pennsylvania. Of course, this was going to be a general séance, not just about the house. As a result, the medium was able to tell some of my students things about their personal lives which she could not have known." Shaner also brought some of the things that used to belong to his late aunt, Annie Bouchart, and put them on the table. One of the students got hold of a skull from his father's dentistry school and placed that on the table, too. The reason why Shaner thought his aunt's property might induce the medium to make a contact was not altogether a question of spirit communication. Shaner's aunt had had the reputation of being a witch, a Pennsylvania Dutch witch, that is. Annie, whose married name was Beavert, was apparently a very colorful person. Old-timers in the area used to say that when people went to visit her and she wanted them to leave, she would manage to have the iron plates on her wooden stove pop up into the air and dance. Several people told Shaner that they had actually seen this.

"People said my aunt could do more than eat bread, which is a nice way of saying she was a witch," Shaner commented. He then showed me some of the books his aunt had left him. Among them were *The Housefriend*, *The Forbidden Friend*, and several other occult books published in the first half of the nineteenth century. Shaner had bought the farm his aunt once owned but later sold it again because he couldn't get electricity to the property. On the farm, he found wishbones nailed all over the wagon sheds, and strange writings in what looked like Hebrew but which made no sense in that language.

Bringing down his aunt's books and other personal belongings apparently pleased the spirit of the late Mrs. Beavert. A rocking chair which had once belonged to her and now stood in the dining room of the house rocked of its own volition all through the evening, although no one sat in it. One of the students had come to look at it and sat in it, but when the chair wouldn't stop even though he wanted it to, he got out of it and ran. According to the medium, the aunt was present all right, and she wanted Shaner to know that she was looking after his well-being. Since Shaner wasn't married yet at the time, that seemed only right on the part of a friendly aunt. Eventually, the medium got around to the house itself. The room had now been darkened, and everybody had quieted down. "We were all pretty psyched up," Shaner recalled, "waiting for things to happen." In addition to the students, the newspaper reporter, Shaner, and his intended, some friends had also joined the group.

After a while, the medium said she saw a young woman in a long gown walking through the house, weeping because she was so happy it was being restored. Next she described a well-dressed tall man coming into the sitting room and taking off his traveling coat. Then she "saw" a large dog with short hair, unlike any of the Shaner dogs, roaming through the house. Finally she described a lackey of very short stature walking through the center hall.

Shortly after the first séance, Shaner received an inquiry from an attorney in New Jersey concerning Betsy Lesher, the Colonel's last child. Apparently, there was no genealogical record of her in American literature. Sometime after receiving this letter, Shaner was lying half-asleep on his bed when he heard a little girl recite a poem in a sassy voice: "Twinkle, twinkle, little star, I wonder how you shine?" Obviously, the little girl didn't know her poem too well. Later, when Shaner undertook historical regression experiments with some of his students, he was to discover that one of the rooms upstairs, now called the reading room, had allegedly been used as Betsy's bedroom, which she shared with her grandmother.

Shaner and his fiancée were so delighted with the first séance that they decided to have another session. The medium suggested that a hypnotist come along to put her under so that she could go into deep trance. This was in the spring of 1970. The hypnotist turned out to be Barrie Schlenker, who is known as a professional magician, working under the name of Barrett the Magician. Like most magicians, Barrie Schlenker was more concerned with uncovering "fraudulent mediums" than with the discovery of real psychic phenomena. Nevertheless, he accepts historical regression as a valid form of research and is also a minister in the Church of Spiritual Revelations, which he describes as a "spiritualist-type religion." Young Schlenker makes his home in Lehighton, Pennsylvania, and once had his own television series, "The Magic Castle." But his presence at the séance made Mrs. Terrell so self-conscious that she couldn't go into trance *at all*. In order to save the evening, the hypnotist asked if *anyone else* wanted to try to "go under." Shaner's brother-in-law, John Trout, who happened to be visiting unexpectedly, volunteered. Just home from the navy, Trout knew nothing about the house or the subject the group was investigating at the time. Fortunately for everyone present, he was a good subject and went into the hypnotic state quickly and easily. Schlenker then took him back into the 1700s.

"And he saw the dining room and described the colors of the woodwork, the exact blue which was under the original paint of the woodwork in the dining room. He described the chandelier and all the furniture," Shaner explained, and one could still see the amazement in his eyes, even though more than a year had gone by. "But one of the most exciting things to me was when we asked John to walk around the entire house *while under hypnosis*. He described wagons coming from Philadelphia and being unloaded; he saw black slaves and white workers; and in particular he described one very hairy man who had on a leather apron." The man John Trout described was unusually large and very muscular —so large, in fact, that the subject gasped while in the hypnotic state. This blonde man was at the forge, loading Conestoga wagons with bar iron. About a year later, while doing research, Shaner happened to come across a letter written by a visiting relative who had been to Colonel Lesher's place in 1914. She vividly described the foreman her great-great-grandfather had had back in the early days and said that he was the strongest man in the country at the time.

The hypnotized brother-in-law went on describing some of the other locations around the place and some buildings which were of great interest to Shaner, because so little was left of them. Trout also described Colonel Lesher in colonial attire, a very tall man with a large dog by his side, and smoking a pipe as he stood in the dining room. Shaner pointed out that his brother-in-law could not have known these details, especially the matter of the paint, since only he, Shaner, had been aware of it. The description of Colonel Lesher's very large dog brought forth a gasp on the part of the Shaners: they had frequently heard the whimper of a dog while in the so-called green bedroom, supposedly Colonel Lesher's own bedroom.

By this time, Shaner was convinced that not only was his aunt Annie interested in his welfare but the late Colonel Lesher was as well. Not that he saw anything unusual in this; after all, had he not with his own hands (and money) restored the Colonel's prize possession? Had he not seen to it that the world knew about Colonel Lesher's interest in national affairs and this part of Pennsylvania in particular? Shaner most certainly had, and if the

Colonel felt he should look after Shaner's affairs, that seemed only right.

After a happy courting period in and around the old forge, Shaner and his present wife were married on April 4, 1970, in the Spangsville Church, the very church Colonel Lesher had favored with a piece of land and had attended as a member of the congregation. Somehow, the date April 4 had suggested itself to the Shaners; it had been set without any particular reason or connection in mind. Later Mrs. Shaner discovered that Colonel Lesher had died on April 4.

Their first child was born on February 10, 1971, and, as is local custom, the church placed a rose on the altar to honor this birth. After the service, the rose was taken from the altar and given to the Shaners, who put it into their dining hall until it faded. But instead of throwing it away, Mrs. Shaner decided to press it and thus preserve it. To that end, she needed some old newspapers. The piece of newspaper she picked to press the flower in was taken at random from a batch of old newspapers given to the Shaners by a neighbor to use in the training of their dog. When Mrs. Shaner checked on the rose a few days later, she was amazed to find that it lay directly underneath the obituary of Shaner's Aunt Annie. The newspaper itself was published in a distant community and would not normally have found its way into the Shaner household. Evidently the Shaner's discarnate friends were working together to let them know that they were keeping in touch.

So impressed were the Shaners with the results of their psychic investigations to date that they decided to continue them in the hope of ferreting out more interesting details about the past of their house. They planned another hypnotic session for the spring of 1971. This time, Shaner decided to bring some of his students to the house, especially those who had shown a certain aptitude for E.S.P. The session was an absolute success. One of the students, Ed Smith, a good hypnotic subject, was sent back into the 1770s, just as Shaner's brother-in-law had been before. In the hypnotic state, he was made to walk through the house and to describe what he saw. Among other things, young Smith described a fireplace in Shaner's bedroom and said that it had been walled over but that no one knew about it. He also described what he thought was a spear, and later, after he had come out of hypnosis, he made a drawing of it. The drawing showed the handle of a colonial pump, an object the student had never seen before. All in all, four students took part in the experiment. One student turned out to be a poor subject, but two girls named Pat Hare and Kathy McCann went under simultaneously. Both of them saw almost the same things while under hypnosis yet had not had an opportunity to talk to each other before the session. Pat described an unusual piece of furniture—a typical eighteenth-century piece used for storing clothes—of which she could not have had any knowledge in her waking condition. The subject was asked to read the date on the furniture, and after some difficulty she came up with the year 1748.

"But I was also interested in treasure, since Colonel Lesher was a wealthy man and might have had some secret hiding place," Shaner continued. In response, Pat said there was a trap door in one corner leading to a lower floor. The hypnotist, Barrie, suggested that she open it and go down. The subject then described a corridor tall enough to stand up in. In this corridor she walked for about twenty-five feet, bearing to the left and then into a cave area ten feet in diameter, where she described boxes of guns and ammunition. She described the guns as Kentucky long rifles and then explained that Colonel Lesher had ordered the corridor filled up. Why had the Colonel filled up the secret passage? Shaner

A Visit to Oley Forge

wanted to know. Lesher's son John, according to the subject, was taking his girlfriends into the secret passageway, and the Colonel didn't like it. His own men did the job, using stone and rubble, and filled the passage completely. However, when the subject was asked to point out the location of the secret passage, she could not do so. At the time, Shaner did not insist on pursuing that line of questioning, eager to learn more about the history of his house and, in particular, which member of Lesher's family had used which room.

Sometimes historical research can become quite hot in more ways than one. "When Pat was upstairs, the hypnotist asked her to describe what she saw," Shaner continued, "and she said that a boy and a girl were playing at the end of the hallway. The hypnotist asked, 'Well, what bedroom are they in?' and Pat replied that they were near the yellow bedroom. This is what we now call the northwest bedroom. Then the hypnotist asked, 'Whose bedroom is that?' and the subject replied, 'John's bedroom.' The hypnotist continued, asking, 'What are they doing now?' and Pat replied that John and the girl had stripped and had gone into bed. The hypnotist, realizing that she was embarrassed, asked how old they were, and she said the girl was twenty and John was nineteen. Both girls were very, uh . . . refined, and by no stretch of the imagination would they have conjured up such a story."

Pat also mentioned under hypnosis that Colonel Lesher's son George slept across the hall. Shaner found out that Lesher had no son named George but did have a son-in-law by that name. This, of course, would not have been known to the subject.

But Pat Hare was able to give the investigators even more interesting details from the past. During the session with the medium, Mrs. Terrell, it had developed that there was a small room upstairs with just two chairs in it, and that these chairs would always move around "by themselves." At the time, the

Shaners had been planning to develop this particular room into a sitting room, to read in. Pat Hare was not present during that first séance and thus had no knowledge of the medium's remarks. However, under hypnosis she mentioned the very same small room upstairs and the two chairs, and explained that it was once the bedroom of Colonel Lesher's mother-in-law. The youngest child, Betsy, had lived in it and had slept there with her grandmother. "We were surprised to have a ghost in the house who could move chairs, and especially surprised that it could be Betsy Lesher," Shaner explained.

"Mr. Shaner," I said, "why would Colonel Lesher have arms and ammunition stored away in a secret hiding place?"

"He was one of George Washington's suppliers of guns," Shaner replied. "As a matter of fact, we discovered the foundation of a building buried in rubble, and when we excavated it, it yielded a hidden corridor. We have not been able to complete the excavation of this corridor, but so far we have found a coin dated 1750, a halfpenny of George II."

Because Pat Hare had proven to be such a good hypnotic subject, another session was held with her as the chief subject a little later. During the second session, she was able to pinpoint the exact location of the hidden corridor, thus enabling Shaner and his helpers to unearth it. It had been sealed in 1777.

That the storage room had to be secret did not surprise me. At that time, Pennsylvania was very much divided between Revolutionaries and Tories. Allentown, which is only a short distance from Oley, was completely in Tory hands, and the area around Oley contained many wealthy farmers, most of them Tories. But Colonel Lesher was on the side of the Yankees even before the Declaration of Independence.

"Pat Hare spoke also of a servant being intercepted with a letter prior to the Declaration of Independence in July 1776,"

Shaner commented. "She mentioned the trial of the Colonel's servant about March 1776. According to the hypnotized subject, the servant was tried by a 'kangaroo court,' found guilty of treason, and executed."

"Did anything else of significance come out under hypnosis?" I asked.

"Yes, one more interesting thing. We asked Pat, under hypnosis, whom Colonel Lesher had liked most during his time. She replied that he had liked a fellow named Stiegel because he made such fine glass. I was, of course, very excited because Stiegel glass was the first American-made glass and is considered very valuable today. In fact, most museums have samples of it. Since I like antiques myself, I asked her, 'What did Colonel Lesher do with his Stiegel glass?' She replied that he threw it down into the well. Later on, I had some of my students doing archeological work, and we managed to dig up the Colonel's old privy, which was nothing but a stone-lined hole going down about six feet. Conceivably it could have been the "well" Pat saw, for we found pieces of genuine Stiegel glass in it."

With that, Shaner showed me some of the pieces of glass he and his team had found in the Colonel's privy. Digging old toilets is standard procedure with most antiquity buffs, especially those who purchase colonial houses. Apparently, when they reached a level of three feet under the surface, they found the rest of the privy filled with nothing but Colonel Lesher's broken china and glassware.

In the same hypnotic session, one of the students claimed that Betsy Ross of Philadelphia had been present in Colonel Lesher's house on January 5, 1777. When the hypnotist asked her why on that date, she explained that she had come to celebrate the Colonel's birthday (which happens to be January 5, according to historical records).

Various people staying at the house have heard strange noises that they could not explain on ordinary grounds. There was Barry Warke, seventeen, who stayed in the green room at the head of the stairs. He never wanted to stay in that room again. Later, a photographer from New York who came to visit the Shaners was given the same room; he, too, heard strange noises of *something* in the fireplace. Neither man could get any sleep in the green bedroom. That was the room in which Shaner had heard an invisible dog whimper.

"Any unusual dreams?" I asked.

"Well, in the winter of 1970–1971 I had an unusual dream in which I saw myself living in the 1700s and seeing all the forges and furnaces as they were then. I vividly remember the roof line and the water wheels that were turning the bellows, and in the morning I couldn't get over how vivid the dream had been. It was almost like watching a motion picture. A few days later, I was impressed to go down to the cellar after supper and dig. I hadn't been doing any digging in the cellar since we had come to the house, and I didn't know the reason why I should suddenly go down into the cellar, but I had a strong compulsion to do so. It was as if I were being led right to one wall, and at that spot I actually dug up a colonial plate in almost perfect condition. This sort of thing has been happening to me in dreams. We have had great insight into the restoration of the house, and it all seems to be something which is unraveling through an understanding which I did not have before."

"Do you think someone is guiding you?"

"It almost seems that way. You see, I am dealing in an area of which very few people know anything—colonial forges and furnaces. Whenever I need to go over some technical terms to double-check them, it just seems as though someone is helping me. Also, I have always wanted a covered wagon for my place, but

A Visit to Oley Forge

they are very rare in this area. Last winter, by pure chance, if it be that, a friend of mine informed me that a covered wagon was standing at an antique dealer's nearby, and I was able to buy it for very little money."

"What role did this house play during the Revolutionary War?"

"Colonel Lesher, being Pennsylvania Dutch and bilingual, served as a liaison man between the Pennsylvania Dutch in this county and Philadelphia. And of course he supplied General Washington's army with matériel."

Before coming here, I had already decided to test my own reactions to the house and to see whether Sherry Wright would feel something in the atmosphere as well, since she had had some psychic experiences in the past. I had carefully noted my impressions and thought the time had come to check them out with the owner of the house.

"My first impression," I said to Shaner, "as I walked in here, that is, into this room, was that I was sitting in on a major dinner party of some sort with a number of people in uniform, toasting some special occasion. I have the feeling that there are at least thirteen or fourteen men here. One of the uniforms seems to be blue and white. They wear wigs, and the occasion has something to do with a victory of sorts. It has not been fought in this area but somewhere else, yet the news has just come in, and I have the feeling that it happened either in this room or in the kitchen next to it. Any comment?"

"Well," Shaner replied, "Pat Hare, under hypnosis, stated that Colonel Lesher wore a powder blue coat, and of course he always wore his white wig. Also, according to this historical hypnosis experiment, there had been a battalion of men here who were very nicely uniformed. As far as any particular toast is concerned, I can only say that we dug some champagne glasses out of the privy."

I continued to recount my impressions. "When we were upstairs in the corner bedroom, I had the feeling of a wedding parlor of sorts and of the marriage of two important families. It was my impression that two important pieces of land were merged with that particular union. The young man was ready to join someone's army, ready to go away shortly. I felt a sense of tragedy. After he left, he was wounded, and then he retired from public life."

Richard Shaner had listened to my account with great interest. "As far as marriage is concerned, other than Colonel Lesher himself, there was his son Jacob, whom I hadn't mentioned to you before. Jacob married a girl from the Trexler family, and both families were huge landholders. Almost half of Allentown comes from the Trexler family, for instance. They also owned iron forges and furnaces, so it was a most successful merger. Jacob was living here at the time, so it stands to reason that they would have had the reception here."

"Did he serve in any armed forces?"

"No, he didn't, and it is a strange thing indeed. Colonel Lesher was extremely patriotic and served, and yet his son supposedly stayed back to run the business. It seems very peculiar."

"The initial 'F' for Frederick came to mind also."

"Yes . . . that would be Frederick Spange. He owned the forge after Colonel Lesher."

"Was he by any chance a very angry man, very short tempered?"

"Probably. This mansion we are in now wasn't good enough for him. He built a very elegant mansion down the road and used this only as an all-purpose house for the foreman."

"Is there an Elizabeth connected with this house?"

"Yes, Colonel Lesher's daughter, and possibly the historical Elizabeth Ross."

A Visit to Oley Forge [169]

I then turned to Sherry and asked her to record her impressions of various parts of the house. "Going up the stairs," she said, "I felt a little sad, and when I got to the bedroom at the top of the stairs, the bathroom especially was magnetic, more than the other half of the room."

"In reference to the bathroom," Shaner commented, "it was cut out of the room that was supposedly Elizabeth Lesher's and her mother-in-law's. The room was L-shaped, so if you had two beds, one of them would have been where the bathroom is now. As for the staircase giving you a special feeling, that is interesting too. My sister once saw a light come down the staircase. It looked like a candle being carried down the stairs by a woman. The house was in total darkness at the time."

Night was falling fast over Oley Valley. I thanked the Shaners for a pleasant visit and asked Sherry to drive us to Philadelphia, which at that time, luckily, was no longer occupied by the British.

11

The Lady from Long Island

Maurice O. is an elderly man of Polish extraction, healthy, vigorous, and strong, despite his years. He is firmly rooted in the Roman Catholic faith but is also aware of the psychic world around him. Mr. O. operates a workshop located in a loft occupying the second story of a house on lower Broadway. The section is one of the oldest parts of New York City. This case was brought to my attention by the man's nephew, a teacher on Long Island who had developed an interest in historical research, especially research pertaining to the American Revolutionary period.

When I met Mr. O., he was at first very suspicious of me and my psychic friend, Ingrid Beckman. He didn't understand what parapsychology was or what we were going to do in his place.

Patiently, I explained that I wanted Ingrid to get her bearings and to see whether she could pick up something from "the atmosphere." While Ingrid was puttering around in the rear of the place, I convinced Mr. O. that I had to know what had happened to him, so that I could judge the case fairly. He explained that he had been in the neighborhood for fifty-five years. He remembered that, when he was a small boy, another building had stood on the same spot. "I came here from Poland in 1913, when I was ten years old," Mr. O. explained in a halting, heavily accented voice. "In this spot there was an old building, a red brick building with few windows. On the corner there was a United cigar store. Down the block was a saloon. They had girls there; customers could come into the saloon, have the girls, and go upstairs with them. In those days it cost them fifty cents or a dollar. There also used to be a barber shop in the building. In 1920 they tore down the old building and built the present factory loft, but they used the same foundations."

When Mr. O. moved his business into a building he had known all his life, it was a little like a homecoming for him. He was in the business of servicing high-speed sewing machines, which were sent to him from all over the country. Most of the time he did the work alone; for a while, his brother Frank had assisted him. In those days he never gave psychic phenomena any thought, and the many strange noises he kept hearing in the loft didn't really bother him. He thought there must be some natural explanation for them, although there were times when he was sure he heard heavy footsteps going up and down the stairs when he was alone in the building. One Saturday afternoon around four o'clock, as he was ready to wash up and go home, he walked back into the shop to wipe his hands. All of a sudden he saw a heavy iron saw fly up into the air on its own volition. It fell down to the floor, broken in two.

Mr. O. picked up the pieces and said to nobody in particular, "Ghost, come here. I am not afraid of you; I want to talk to you." However, there was no answer.

"See that latch on the door," Maurice O. said to us, and showed us how he locked the place so that nobody could come in. "Many times I've seen that latch move up and down, as if someone wanted to get in, and when I went outside there was no one there."

Oftentimes he would hear footsteps overhead in the loft above his. When he would go upstairs to check what the noise was all about, he would find the third-floor loft solidly locked up and no one about. Once, when he went to the toilet between 1:30 and 2:00 P.M., at a time when he knew he was alone in the building, he found himself locked out of his place, yet he knew he had left the door open. Someone, nevertheless, had locked the latch *from the inside*. Finally, with the help of a friend, he broke the door open and of course found the place empty. The incident shook Mr. O. up considerably, as he couldn't explain it, no matter how he tried. During this time, too, he kept seeing shadows, roughly in the shape of human beings. They would move up and down in the back of his workshop and were of a grayish color. "It was the shape of a banana," Mr. O. commented. Curiously, during the first eight years of his occupancy—he had been across the street for forty years before—Mr. O. had had no such problems. It was only in the last two years that he began to notice things out of the ordinary.

However, Mr. O. had heard rumors of strange goings-on in the building. A previous owner of the loft building had a music store and was in the habit of spending Saturday nights in his shop with some invited friends, listening to music. One night, so the story goes, around midnight, everything started to pop out of the shelves, merchandise flying through the air, and the entire building began to shake as if there had been an earthquake. While all this was going on, the people in the music store heard a tremendous noise overhead. They became frightened and called the police. Several radio cars responded immediately but could not find out what was wrong. Everything seemed normal upstairs. Shortly after, the owner sold the building and moved to California.

Mr. O.'s workshop is L-shaped, with a small office immediately behind the heavy steel door that gives access to the corridor, and thence to a steep staircase that leads out into the street. The machine shop itself is to the left and in back of the office. Thus, it is possible to work in the back of the shop and not see anyone coming in through the entrance door. But it is not possible to escape hearing any noises on the floor, since the entire building is not very large.

The day after Thanksgiving 1971 Maurice was alone in the shop, working quietly on some orders he wanted to get out of the way. Since it was the day after Thanksgiving and just before the weekend, the building was very quiet. There was no one upstairs, and Maurice was sure he was the only one in the building at the time. Suddenly, he saw a lady walk into his office. Since he had not heard the heavy door slam, which it always does when someone walks in, he wondered how she had gotten into the building and into his office. She wore what to Maurice seemed a very old-fashioned, very chic dress, white gloves, and a bonnet, and she smelled of a sweet fragrance that immediately captured him. What was so nice a lady doing in his sewing machine shop?

Maurice did not pursue his line of thought, how she had gotten in in the first place, but asked her what she wanted. Somehow, he felt a little frightened. He had noticed that her face was more like a skeleton covered with skin than the face of a flesh-and-blood person. The lady seemed unusually white. There was no reply; she simply stood there, looking around the place. Maurice repeated his question.

"Well," she said finally, in a faraway tone of voice, "I just came here to look at the place. I used to live in this building." Then she went to the window and pointed to the street. "I used to play over there—these houses are all new brick houses. My father and mother had a corn farm where the Federal Building is now, downtown."

"Was there anything peculiar about her tone of voice?" I asked.

"No, it sounded pretty clear to me, real American," O. replied. "She said, 'You know, all these new buildings weren't here during Revolutionary times.' Then she added, rather apologetically, 'I just came around to look.'"

Maurice was standing in back of the counter that separates his office from the short stretch of corridor leading from the entrance door. The lady was standing on the other side of the counter, so Maurice could get a good look at her; but he was too frightened to look her in the face. When he backed up, she started to talk rapidly. "I just wanted to visit the neighborhood. I used to live here." Then, pointing her hand toward the window, she said, "The headquarters of the British Army used to be across the street."

The statement made no impression on Mr. O. Besides, he was much too upset by all this to wonder how a woman standing before him in the year 1971 could remember the location of the headquarters of the British Army, which had left New York almost two hundred years before.

"What did she look like?" I asked.

"She was dressed very nicely, and she looked just like any other person except for her face. I didn't see her hands, but she had on brand new gloves, her dress looked new, and the hat was real nice."

"Did you see her walking?"

"Yes, she was walking."

"What happened next?"

"Well," Maurice explained, swallowing hard at the memory of his experience, "I finally got up enough courage to ask her, 'Where are you going now?' "

The question had seemed to make the lady sad, even upset. "I'm leaving to visit relatives on Long Island," she said finally. "In the cemetery. My relatives, my friends, my father and mother."

Maurice became more and more uneasy at all this. He pretended that he had some business in the rear of the shop and started to back up from the counter.

"I'm going to visit you again," the lady said and smiled.

For about a minute, Mr. O. busied himself in the back of his workshop, then returned to the office. The woman was gone.

"Was the door still closed?"

"The door was closed. No one could have left without slamming this door, and I would have heard it. I quickly opened the door to convince myself that I had really spoken to a person. I looked around; there was nobody outside. Nobody."

Maurice checked both his door and the door downstairs. Neither door had been opened, so he went back up to continue working. He was still very much upset but decided to stay till about five o'clock. When he was ready to go home and had put the keys into the door, he suddenly began to smell the same perfume again—the perfume the lady had brought with her. She's back again, he thought, and he looked everywhere. But there was no one about. Quickly he locked the door and ran downstairs.

A year to the day after the apparition, Maurice decided to work late—more out of curiosity than out of any conviction that she would return. But the lady never did.

Mr. O.'s nephew, who is a teacher and a researcher, commented, "With reference to the British headquarters' being across the street, I have checked this fact out and have found that during the Revolution the British headquarters *were* across the street from this same building my uncle now occupies. This is a fact I know my uncle couldn't possibly have known."

"Ingrid," I said, after I had asked her to join me and Mr. O. in the front of the workshop, "what do you feel about this place?"

"There is a lot of excitement here," she replied. "I think there is a man here who is kind of dangerous, very treacherous, and I think someone might have been injured here. This happened about twenty-five years ago."

"Do you think there is an earlier presence in this house?"

"I feel that this was a prosperous place, an active, busy spot. A lot of people were coming here. It was part home, part business. Before that I think this building was something else. I think a family lived here. They may have been foreigners, and I think the man was killed. I feel that this man came to this country and invested his savings here. He wanted to build up a family business. I also think there is a woman connected with it. She wears a longish dress, going below the knees."

"What is her connection with this place?"

"She may have spent her childhood here—what happened here might have happened to her father. Perhaps she came here as a young child and spent many years in this building. She has some connection with this man, I feel."

"Does she have any reason to hang onto this place?"

"Maybe she doesn't understand why all this has happened, and she can't accept it yet. Perhaps she has lost a loved one."

The Lady from Long Island

Every year, around Thanksgiving, Maurice O. will wait for the lady to come back and talk to him again. Now that he knows that she is "just a ghost," he isn't even afraid of her any longer. As far as the lady is concerned, she need not worry either: when the British Army headquarters stood across the street, the area was a lot safer than it is now, especially at night; but she really needn't worry about muggings either, things being as they are.